Wolfred Nelson Cote

Baptism and Baptisteries

Wolfred Nelson Cote

Baptism and Baptisteries

ISBN/EAN: 9783743330771

Manufactured in Europe, USA, Canada, Australia, Japa

Cover: Foto ©ninafisch / pixelio.de

Manufactured and distributed by brebook publishing software (www.brebook.com)

Wolfred Nelson Cote

Baptism and Baptisteries

BAPTISM

AND

BAPTISTERIES.

BY
WOLFRED NELSON COTE,
MISSIONARY IN ROME.

PHILADELPHIA:
THE BIBLE AND PUBLICATION SOCIETY,
530 ARCH STREET.

TO THE

Southern Baptist Convention

THIS BOOK IS

AFFECTIONATELY DEDICATED

BY

THE AUTHOR.

ALPHABETICAL LIST

OF THE

PRINCIPAL AUTHORS CONSULTED IN THIS WORK.

ANASTASIUS BIBLIOTHECARIUS. *De vitis Romanorum pontificum, cum notis Blanchinii.* 4 vol. in-fol. 1718-1723.
ARINGHI. *Roma subterranea.* In-f°. 2 vol. Romæ, 1651-1659.
BERNARDINUS FERRARIUS. *De ritu sacrarum Ecclesiæ veteris concionum, cum præfatione Joanni Georgii Grævii.* Veronæ, 1731. In-4°.
BERTOLI FRANCESCO. *Notizie delle Pitture ecc. d' Italia.*
BERTOLUZZI. *Nuoviss. Guida della Città di Parma.*
BIANCONI. *Della Chiesa del s. Sepolcro di Bologna.*
BIBLIOTHECA MAGNA VETERUM PATRUM ET ANTIQUORUM SCRIPTORUM ECCLESIASTICORUM. 1644.
BLANCHINIUS *Demonstratio historiæ ecclesiasticæ comprobatæ monumentis pertinentibus ad fidem temporum et gestorum.* Romæ, 1752. 3 tom. in-f°.
BOLDETTI. *Osservazioni sopra i cimiteri de' santi martiri ed antichi Cristiani di Roma.* In-f°. Roma, 1720.
BOTTARI. *Sculture e pitture sagre estratte dai cimiteri di Roma, pubblicate già dagli autori della Roma sotterranea, ed' ora nuovamente date in luce colle spiegazioni.* Roma, 3 vol. in-f°. 1737-1754.

LIST OF AUTHORS.

MARTENE. *De antiquis Ecclesiæ ritibus.* 4 vol. in-f°. Venetiis, 1783.
MARTINI. *Theatrum Basilicæ Pisanæ.* Romæ, 1728.
MORONI. *Dizionario di erudiz. storico-ecclesiast.*
OLEARII (J. Gothofr.). *Bibliotheca scriptorum ecclesiasticorum.* Ienæ, 1711. 2 vol. in-4°.
PACIAUDI. 1° *De cultu S. Joannis Baptistæ.* In-4°. Romæ, 1755. 2° *De sacris Christianorum balneis.* In 4°. Romæ, 1758.
RASPONI (Cæs.). *De basilica et patriarch. Lateranensi.* Romæ, 1656. In-f°.
ROSSI (J. B. DE'.) 1° *Inscriptiones Christianæ urbis Romæ septimo sæculo antiquiores.* 2° *De Christianis monumentis* IX⊖TN *exhibentibus.* 3° *Roma sotteranea Cristiana.*
SALIG. *De diptychis veterum.*
SCHELSTRATE. *Antiquitatis Ecclesiæ dissertationibus, monumentis ac notis illustratæ libri tres.* Romæ, 1692. In-f°.
SELVAGGIO. *Antiquitatum Christianarum institutiones.* Vercellis, 1778. 6 vol. in-12°.
TOMASI. *Institutiones theologicæ antiquorum Patrum.* Romæ, 1705 seqq. 2 vol. in-4°.
VISCONTI (Pietro). *Sposizione di alcune antiche iscrizioni Cristiane.* Roma, 1824. In-8°.
WEIDLING (C. W.). *De baptisteriis veterum Christianorum.* Lips., 1737. In-4°.
ZACCARIA (Fr. Ant.). 1° *Raccolta di dissertazioni di storia ecclesiastica.* Roma, 22 vol. in-8°. 1792-1797. 2° *Bibliotheca ritualis.* Romæ, 1776. 3 vol. in-4°. 3° *De veterum Christianarum inscriptionum usu in rebus theologicis.* Romæ.
ZIEGLER (Gaspar.). *De diaconis et diaconissis veteris Ecclesiæ.* Wittebergæ, 1688. In-4°.

All the above works, and the writings of the Fathers, may be consulted at the Biblioteca Casanatense, a library attached to the convent of the Dominicans, and which is the richest in Rome in printed works. It is composed of one hundred and twenty thousand volumes, and contains a valuable collection of ancient manuscripts.

ILLUSTRATIONS.

Baptistery in Catacomb of S. Ponziano. *Frontispiece.*
Baptism of a Convert by Cyril 57
Benediction of the Font 58
Russian Baptism 62
Section of Frigidarium of Bath, Pompeii 107
Plan of Frigidarium 108
Plan of Baptistery of Constantine, Rome 115
Plan of Baptistery of S. Costanza, Rome 120
Plan of Baptistery at Nocera dei Pagani 124
Section and Plan of Baptistery at Citta Nuova . . 136
Plan of Baptistery at Florence 141
Interior of Baptistery at Florence 142
Plan of Baptistery at Verona 147
Section of Baptistery at Verona 147

ILLUSTRATIONS.

Plan of Baptistery at Cremona 150

Baptistery at Cremona 151

Plan of Cathedral and Baptistery of Torcello . . . 152

Baptistery of Pisa 154

Plan of Baptistery of Pisa 155

Baptism of Christ in Jordan, Parma, thirteenth century 162

Baptism and Baptisteries.

PART I.

BAPTISM.

THE natural tendency of the human mind is to adopt a physical and outward act, as a sign, figure, symbol, or representation of an inward and spiritual effect. This tendency has always been strong, especially in the earlier and ruder states of society. The purification of the body by water, for example, has, in all ages and in all religions, been considered as an emblem fitted to express that purity of the soul with which man should approach the

Deity, and has been therefore adopted as an important religious ceremony.

Ablution was one of the principal rites of initiation to the worship of Mithra, a goddess held in high veneration by the Persians. The Egyptians appear to have practised it from the earliest antiquity. Herodotus, in the 2d Book of his History, chapter xxxvii., informs us that the priests of Isis and Osiris bathed twice during the day in cold water, and as often in the night. Those initiated to the sacred mysteries of these divinities were bathed in water by the priests. The annual festival of Isis lasted eight days, during which a general purification took place.

The use of water in religious rites was known to the ancient Greeks, who employed it under various forms. No one could be admitted to the Eleusinian mysteries until he had been plunged in the waters of the river Ilissus, consecrated to the Muses. Hesychius (*In Eleusin*) says that the priest whose office was to purify thus the initiated, was called ὑδρανος, or the *waterer*. He also informs us that the Greeks used to plunge in water the infants and those who had been in danger of death; hence these were called δευτερόποτ-μοι, or ὑστερόποτμοι. Reference is made to the pagan baptisms by Clemens Alexandrinus,* in the 5th Book of his *Stromata*, and Tertullian,† in his *Præscriptionibus*, c. xl., and *De Baptismo*, c. v.

Ovid, Virgil, and Juvenal make frequent allusions in their writings ‡ to the *aqua lus-*

---

* Clemens, a converted philosopher and presbyter of Alexandria, who died about A. D. 218. He is esteemed the most profoundly learned of the Fathers of the church. He is the author of several important works, amongst them the *Protrepticon* (προτρεπτικὸς λόγος), or *Exhortation to the Gentiles;* the *Pædagogus*, or a treatise on Christianity; the *Institutes;* and the *Stromata*, or Miscellany, in eight books.

† Tertullian, a celebrated Father of the church; died about A. D. 220; has left a great variety of tracts on the vices and customs of his age. Author of an Apology, of a work against Marcion, and of a treatise on Baptism.

‡ Est locus, in Tyberim, quo lubricus influit almo,
   Et nomen magno in amne minor,

tralis, or water of purification, used in the religious ceremonies of the ancient Romans, who were scrupulous in employing it before they performed a sacrifice. It was commonly placed at the entrance of the temple, and sprinkled upon the worshipers as they entered, with a small olive branch. A vessel containing it was also placed in the *forum*, for the use of the citizens assembled there. This lustration was administered at the termination of the funeral rites, to remove the defilement supposed to be contracted by approaching a dead body. According to Theodoret (Hist. Eccles., lib. iii., c. xiv.),* it was usual to sprinkle water over the food served up at the *epulæ*, or solemn religious repasts.

 Illuc purpurea canus cum Veste sacerdos,
 Almonis dominam sacraque lavit aquis.
        Ovid, *In Fast.*, 4.
 Spargens rore levi et ramo felicis olivæ
 Lustravitque viros.—Virgil, *Æneid*, 6.
 Portabit aquas ut sparget in æde
 Isidis.—Juvenal, *Satyr*, 6.

  * *Encyclopædia Metropolitana.*

It is well known that all the oriental religions abound with ablutions. The Syrians, Copts, etc., have their annual solemn washings. The Mohammedans practise ablutions most punctiliously, and in the greatest number. The superstitious attachment of the Hindoos for the river Ganges is such, that ablution in its streams is placed among the first duties of religion; and when, from necessity, they cannot reach that river, if, in bathing, they use the exclamation, " O Ganges, purify me!" the Brahmins assure them that the service is equally efficacious.*

In accordance with divine directions, the Jews introduced into their religious rites the use of the water of purification, made with the ashes of a heifer (Numbers ix.). Several other ceremonies of the Mosaic law were accompanied by ablutions. Bathing in water is said by some Jewish authors to have been used, together with circumcision, in the ad-

---

* *Encyclopædia Metropolitana.*

mission of proselytes. These were required to renounce idolatry and believe in Jehovah, were interrogated while standing in the water, and after baptism were declared to be clean and holy, and were admitted to all the privileges of the Jewish nation. As the sacred writers make no mention of this custom, nor is there any reference to it in the best Targums, in the apocryphal books, in the writings of Josephus and Philo, nor in the Fathers of the first three centuries, it is probable, if not in fact certain, that this rite was introduced only after the destruction of Jerusalem, when the sacrifices had ceased. This custom still exists; Leo of Modena, Rabbi of Venice, says in his book *De Ritibus et Usis Judæorum*, pars i. c. 3, "He who desires to become a Jew is first circumcised, and a few days after is entirely bathed in water in presence of three Rabbis who have examined him. He is then considered a Jew like the others."

The introduction of John's baptism was, to a certain degree, in harmony with the long established usages of the Jews—the frequency of lustrations which constituted a part of the Mosaic ceremonial, and were practised on various occasions both by the priests and by the people. Ablution in the waters of the river Jordan was well fitted to represent the washing away of sins through repentance and faith in the coming Messiah, the Lamb of God, who was to take away the sin of the world.

When our Saviour entrusted to his disciples the great commission, he instituted baptism as one of the peculiar rites of his church and kingdom. "All power is given unto me in heaven and in earth. Go ye, therefore, and teach all nations, baptizing them in the name of the Father, and of the Son, and of the Holy Ghost; teaching them to observe all things whatsoever I have commanded you, and lo, I am with you always, even unto the end of the world." And again, "He that believeth and is baptized shall be saved. He that believeth not shall be damned." (Matt. xxviii. 19, 20; Mark xvi. 16.)

In obedience to the divine command, the apostles required of all who received baptism a confession of faith in Christ. The language of Peter on the day of Pentecost to the Jews and Gentiles at Jerusalem was this: "Repent and be baptized every one of you in the name of Jesus Christ for the remission of sins." "They that gladly received the word were baptized," to the number of three thousand. (Acts ii.) When the Holy Ghost fell on all who heard his preaching in the house of Cornelius, Peter said: "Can any man forbid water, that these should not be baptized, which have received the Holy Ghost as well as we?" (Acts x. 47.) When the eunuch requested to be baptized by Philip, his answer was: "If thou believest with all thine heart, thou mayest." (Acts viii. 37.) Thus was fully established Christian baptism, which implied, not only repentance and the washing away of sins, but also faith in a risen Saviour and allegiance to him. It was an outward and visible sign that the convert took upon himself the profession of Christianity. By this act, he renounced his Jewish or Heathen opinions and practices, and adopted the principles of the Christian faith.

Instituted by our Lord as a perpetual ordinance of his religion, baptism is the symbol of his death, burial, and resurrection. It represents, as regards the believer, death to sin and the world, and resurrection to a new life. "Know ye not, that so many of you as were baptized into Jesus Christ, were baptized into his death? Therefore we are buried with him by baptism into death, that like as Christ was raised up from the dead by the glory of the Father, even so we also should walk in newness of life. For if we have been planted together in the likeness of his death, we shall be also in the likeness of his resurrection." (Romans vi. 3–5.) In his comments upon these passages, Justin Martyr * (*Apolog.* ii.) says: "We celebrate in baptism the the symbol and sign of his death and resurrection." Gregory of Nyssa,† in his sermon on repentance, remarks: "The old man is buried in water, the new man is born again, and grows in grace." (*De Pœnitentia*). Chrysostom ‡ says in one of his celebrated Homilies: "By our being

---

* Justin Martyr, a celebrated Greek writer of the second century, and the author of several important works in defence of Christianity. Amongst them may be mentioned his *First Apology*, in which he gives a detail of the manners, rites, and doctrines of the early Christians; his *Second Apology*, which is a complaint of the treatment of the Christians; his *Dialogue with Trypho the Jew*, a work containing various arguments to demonstrate that Jesus was the Messiah.

† Gregory, Bishop of Nyssa, born in A. D. 330. He is the author of several homilies, orations, and letters. His Twelve Books against Eunomius are his best works.

‡ Chrysostom, Bishop of Antioch (354—407), a judicious, eloquent, and energetic expositor of Scripture.

immersed in water, the old man is buried as in a tomb, and in the act of immersion disappears entirely; by our emersion the new man rises from the sepulchre."

Ambrosius* says, in his *De Off.*, iii. c. 4: "In the sacrament of Baptism the whole outer man is buried."

Theodulus, Presbyter of Cœlesyria (died A. D. 490), in his Commentary on the Epistle to the Romans, writes: "As the body of our Lord was buried in the earth, so our body is buried in baptism." Then referring to the custom in his time of immersion repeated three times, he adds: "The three burials and resurrections, typified by the three-fold immersion, symbolize his Death and Resurrection."

---

* Ambrosius (340—397), Archbishop of Milan, a bold defender of the faith, and one of the most celebrated Fathers of the church. He raised his See to such a power that it dared to resist Rome herself, up to the twelfth century. Ambrosius published annotations on Scripture, discourses, and miscellaneous treatises.

Maximus,* in his *Homilia de Juda traditore*, says: "Baptism is to us burial with Christ, in which we die to sin and iniquity; and, the old man being destroyed, we rise again to a new life. It is a burial, by which we lay down our life that we may save it, and receive grace that we may live. Great therefore is the grace of this sepulture, through which a useful death is brought to us, and a still more useful life freely bestowed. Great is the grace of this sepulture with Christ, which purifies the sinner and gives life to the dying."

Gregory the Great:† "We also, when we immerse three times, symbolize the three days of Christ's burial." (*Epist.* lib. i. ep. 43.)

---

* Maximus, Bishop of Turin in the fifth century, and a well known Latin writer.

† Gregory the First was elected Pope in A. D. 590. His chief works are letters, of which there are more than eight hundred. He is also the author of a Commentary on Job, a *Pastorale*, or Treatise on Pastoral Duties, and several Homilies.

Alluding to the words of our Saviour: "For as Jonas was three days and three nights in the whale's belly, so shall the Son of man be three days and three nights in the earth." (Matt. xii. 40.) Alcuinus* says, in his Sixty-ninth Epistle: "The three immersions represent the three nights."

Theodulphus, an ecclesiastical writer of the ninth century, writes in his *De Ordine Baptismi*: "We die to sin when we renounce the devil and all his works; we are buried with Christ when we descend into the font of washing as into a sepulchre and are immersed three times in the name of the Holy Trinity; we rise with Christ when, purified of all our sins, we come out of the font as from a tomb."

---

* Alcuinus, or Albinus, the most distinguished scholar of the eighth century, the confidant and adviser of Charlemagne, and author of numerous works, which consist principally of poems, elementary treatises on the different sciences, letters on a variety of theological subjects, and other works, some of which are lost.

Several allusions to baptism are found among some of the paintings of what Signor De Rossi, in his work "Roma Sotterranea" calls the "Ciclo Biblico," that is, the definite series of purely scriptural subjects represented in many of the Catacombs of Rome, and which belong to an earlier period of Christian Art than those of special saints, martyrs, Bishops of Rome and of other Sees, which are also found there. Thus the Deluge and the Ark of Noah are represented in the Catacombs as symbols of baptism, according to the words of the apostle Peter: "The ark, wherein few, that is, eight souls, were saved by water; the like figure whereunto even baptism doth also now save us, not the putting away of the filth of the flesh, but the answer of a good conscience towards God, by the resurrection of Jesus Christ." (1 Peter iii. 21.) Tertullian expresses himself on this subject in the following terms: "As after the waters of the deluge, in which the old iniquity was purged away, as after that baptism (so to call it) of the old world, a dove sent out of the ark and returning with an olive branch was the herald to announce to the earth peace, and the cessation of the wrath of heaven, so by a similar disposition with reference to matters spiritual, the dove of the Holy Spirit sent out from heaven flies to the earth, that is, to our flesh, as it comes out of the bath of regeneration, after its old sins, and brings to us the peace of God." (*De Baptismo*, vii.)

Another painting, representing a man inclosed in an ark and receiving the olive branch from the mouth of the dove, painted upon the walls of a chapel in the catacombs, was intended to show that the faithful, having obtained the remission of their sins through faith in Christ and baptism, had received from the Holy Spirit the gift of divine peace, and are saved in the mystical ark of Christ from the destruction which awaits the world.

And if the same picture be rudely scratched on a single tomb, it denotes the same fact and the hope of the survivors that the deceased, being a faithful servant of Christ and a member of his body, had died in the peace of God and had now entered into his rest.

The passage of the Red Sea was also represented as a figure of baptism, in accordance with the words of the apostle Paul: "Moreover, brethren, I would not that ye should be ignorant how that all our fathers were under the cloud, and all passed through the sea, and were all baptized unto Moses in the cloud and in the sea." (1 Cor. x. 1, 2.) In his thirty-ninth sermon, Gregory of Nazianzen* says: "Moses truly baptized in

---

* Gregory of Nazianzen, also called the Theologian, from his erudition in sacred literature, was born A. D. 328, and became one of the first orators, and most accomplished and thoughtful writers of his time. His surviving works consist chiefly of about fifty-three orations, two hundred and forty-two letters, and one hundred and fifty-six poems, besides meditations, descriptions, etc.

water by causing the Israelites to pass through the sea and under the cloud. The sea represents the waters of baptism, and the cloud the Holy Spirit."

Augustine, in his Three hundred and fifty-second Sermon, says: "*Per mare transitus baptismus erat,*" and then, developing this figure, he adds: "The Red Sea typifies baptism; Moses leading through the sea, Christ himself; the Israelites passing through represent the faithful; and the death of the Egyptians, the destruction of our sins." (*De Pœnitentia.*) Prosper, an ecclesiastical writer of the fifth century (*De Promiss.*, pars i. c. 38), the Venerable Bede * (*Quæst. sup.* Exod. xx.), make remarks of a similar character. A picture of the passage of the Red Sea was lately discovered on a sarcophagus of the

---

* Bede (672-735), surnamed the Venerable on account of his learning, piety, and talents. He wrote several theological books, commentaries on the Holy Scriptures, homilies, lives of saints, and an ecclesiastical history of England.

Catacomb of the Vatican, a reproduction of which may be seen in Bottari.* The triumphal arch of Santa Maria Maggiore contains a celebrated mosaic on this subject.

But the symbol to which the Fathers of the church seem to have attached the greatest importance, as bearing directly upon the subjects of baptism and the Lord's Supper, was that of the Fish. In the language of the Christian writers, both in the East and the West, from the second century onwards, our Lord is spoken of as ΙΧΘΥΣ, as " Piscis," " Piscis Noster," and the like, and that for a variety of reasons. First, the fish, blessed to the feeding of great multitudes and of his own disciples, by our Lord himself while on earth, was regarded as a type of that heavenly food which he gave for the life of the world. Secondly, as fish was, in primitive times, very generally in use as an ordinary

---

* Bottari, *Sculture e Pitture sagre Estratte dai Cimiteri di Roma.*

article of food, it served to designate the wholesome doctrine of Christ, and particularly the words of truth contained in Holy Scripture. Thus Jerome,* on Matt. xiv. 17 (*Opp.*, t. iv. p. 60), and again (*ibid.*, t. vii. p. 119), says: "In the seven loaves and the small fishes are found the types of the gospel of Christ. The seven loaves are the seven books of the Old Testament, which we call the Heptateuch, and the small fishes are the smaller books of the New Testament." Clemens Alexandrinus, in his *Stromata* (lib. vi.), speaks of the fishes and barley loaves as typifying the προπαιδεία, or preparatory teaching of the Greeks and the Jews.

This practice of figuratively designating our Lord as ΙΧΘΥΣ, or Piscis, led the Fathers

---

* Jerome (331–420), one of the most learned and eloquent of the Latin Fathers. He translated or revised the *Vulgata;* wrote commentaries on most of the books of Scripture, controversial treatises, and lives and works of preceding ecclesiastical writers. His opinions are often exaggerated and fanciful.

naturally to speak of the waters of baptism. The earliest example of this is the well known passage in Tertullian: "We, smaller fishes, after the example of our Fish, are born in the waters, and it is only by continuing in those waters that we are safe." (*De Baptismo*, c. 1.)

Melito, Bishop of Sardis (about A. D. 160), is the earliest writer who furnishes us with an authority for the application of the term *pisces* to the Christians, when he says: "Fishes are the holy ones of God," *Pisces sancti;* for so it is written: "*Traxerunt rate plenum piscibus magnis,*" John xxi. 11. (*Clavis*, xl. 2.) Elsewhere (cap. xii. n. 25), he refers to the same: "*Centum quinquaginta tres omnes electi.*" Hilary * (*In Matt.*), Opta-

---

* Hilary (305–368), Bishop of Poitiers, occupies an important part in the patristic literature of the Western Church. His most valuable work is that on the Trinity; he wrote also on the Councils, against the Arians, and a commentary on the Psalms and Matthew.

tus* (*De Schism. Donat.*, l. iii. c. 2), and Augustine (*Confessionum*, lib. xiii. c. 23), express the same idea. The second-named writer informs us that the Greek ἰχθύς represents the first letters of "Ἰησοῦς Χριστὸς Θεοῦ Υἱὸς Σωτήρ," "Jesus Christ, Son of God, Saviour," and adds that, owing to the presence in the waters of the Fish, the basin containing the baptismal waters was called "*piscina*," a fishpond.†

A remarkable inscription of great antiquity was discovered a few years ago, buried in the soil of an ancient cemetery in the immediate vicinity of Autun, a town in France, where many ruins of Roman temples, gates,

---

* Optatus, Bishop of Mileri (about A. D. 370), a celebrated ecclesiastical writer.

† The following is the passage referred to: "Hic (*i. e.* Christus) est piscis qui in baptismate per invocationem fontalibus undis inseritur. Cujus piscis nomen secundum appellationem Græcam in uno nomine per singulas literas turbam sanctorum nominum continet ΙΧΘΥΣ, quod est latinum *Jesus Christus Dei Filius Salvator*. (*De Schism. Donat.*, lib. iii. c. 2.)

and triumphal arches still exist. This inscription is of the fourth century, or perhaps of the fifth. Is is a sepulchral one, in memory of a certain Pectorius, a son of Aschandeius, and seems to have been placed near the baptistery of a church, and to have been designed as an invitation, first, to receive the ordinance of baptism, and next, to partake with earnest desire and devout reverence of the Lord's Supper. This inscription begins as follows:

ἸΧΘΥΟΣ οὐρανίου . . . . . γένος, ἦτορι σεμνῷ,

and has been translated thus:

"O thou offspring of the Heavenly Ichthus (Christ), use with a reverent heart when thou hast received the immortal fountain of Divine Waters among mortals. O my friend (who hast been baptized), quicken thy soul with the ever-flowing waters of wealth-giving wisdom. Come and receive the honey-sweet food of the Saviour of the saints. Eat, drink, holding Ichthus in thy hands. Faith brought to us and set before us food, a Fish from a divine font, great and pure, which she took in her hands and gave to her friends, that they should always eat thereof, holding goodly wine, giving with bread a mingled drink. On Ichthus my hands are clasped; in thy love come nigh to me, and be my guide, my Lord and Saviour, O thou Light of the dead."

In the primitive church and up to the sixteenth century, the ordinary mode of baptism was by the immersion of the whole body in water. The original term *baptizo* conveys the meaning of immersion, and no other. On this point we have most valuable testimony from the Fathers of the church, and other ecclesiastical writers. They invariably designate baptism as the act of *dipping, bathing*, or *washing*, and following the language of the apostle Paul, who calls baptism the washing of regeneration (Titus iii. 5), use these two terms as equivalents. Thus Justin

Martyr in his Dialogue with Trypho, the Jew (c. 14), speaking of baptism, says: "By the washing of repentance (διὰ τὸν λουτρὸν τῆς μετανοίας), which God has instituted for the sins of his people, we have understood and affirm this baptism, announced beforehand by Isaiah, and which alone can purify the penitent, to be the Water of Life. For what is the utility of that baptism, by which the body only is cleansed? Let your soul also be purified of all its passions, avarice, envy, and hatred, and lo! the body is pure."

In his First Apology (c. 61), the same writer says: "This washing (λουτρὸν) is called illumination (φώτισμα) on account of the light that enters the minds of those who have been instructed. He who is enlightened is washed in the name of Jesus Christ, crucified under Pontius Pilate, and of the Holy Ghost."

Dionysius, the Areopagite,* in his book,

---

* Dionysius, the Areopagite, was Bishop of Athens in the first century. He is the author of the treatises, *De*

De Ecclesiastica Hierarchia (c. ii.), refers in the following words to trine immersion, that is, immersion repeated three times, which, he says, was done after the three persons of the Godhead: "As Jesus, who is the Prince of Life, remained three days and three nights in the heart of the earth, so the three immersions (τριῶν καταδύσεων) represent the three nights, and the three emersions (ἀναδύσεων) the three days."

Theophilus,* in his second book, *Ad Autolycum*, says: "Men receive remission of sins through the water and the washing of regeneration (διὰ ὕδατὸς καὶ λουτρὸν)."

Irenæus,† in his work *Adversus Hæreses*

Hierarchia Cœleste, De Hierarchia Ecclesiastica, De Nominibus Divinis, and *Mysticæ Theologiæ*.

* Theophilus was Bishop of Antioch in the second century. He wrote three books in defence of the Christian faith, addressed to Autolycus, a learned heathen, with whom he was acquainted.

† Irenæus, Bishop of Lyons, A. D. 170. He was a disciple of Polycarp. His principal work is that which is

(lib. iii. c. 19), speaking of baptism, says: "Our bodies through this washing (lavacrum) have received that which leads to an incorruptible unity."

Tertullian wrote on the subject of baptism a whole treatise to establish the necessity of that ordinance in refutation of the opinion of a female, named Quintilia, who maintained that faith alone (we suppose faith without works) was sufficient for salvation. In this tract, Tertullian, who at times makes use of somewhat exaggerated expressions, speaks strongly of the efficacy of baptism in procuring the remission of sins, and the descent of the Holy Ghost, and connects it with regeneration; he also discusses many questions relating to this rite as practised in his time. In this and other tracts of his, Tertullian

---

commonly cited as *Adversus Hæreses* (Against Heresies), which he wrote in the reign of Commodus, that is, after the year 180. His other works are most of them doctrinal, and are known only by fragments.

makes mention of trine immersion, that is, immersion repeated three times, which, he says, was done after the three persons of the Godhead. "With great simplicity, without any pomp or showy preparations, the candidate is let down into the water, and dipped in each interval between the words (of the formula)." (*De Baptismo, Adversus Quintiliam*, c. 2.) "We affirm before the bishop that we renounce the devil, his pomps, and angels, and are then immersed three times (ter mergitamur)." (*De Corona*, iii.) "We are dipped not once only, but at the name of each person of the Godhead." (*Adversus Praxeas*.)

In the acts of *Perpetua and Felicitas*, who suffered martyrdom in the time of Tertullian, it is said that when one Saturus, a catechumen, was thrown to a leopard in the arena of the Colosseum of Rome, and at the first bite was covered with blood, the people gave him the testimony of the second baptism, as it were, by crying: "*Salvum lotum, salvum lotum.*" Baptized, or more literally, "washed and saved, washed and saved." (*Acta Sanctorum*, lib. i.)

In the *Apostolical Constitutions*, or *Canons*, we find these words: "If any bishop, or presbyter, shall have administered but one immersion, and not three immersions (tres immersiones) at the initiation (baptism), he must be deposed. For our Lord has said, 'Go ye, teach all nations, baptizing them in the name of the Father, and of the Son, and of the Holy Ghost.'" (*Congestum Canones Apostolorum, per Clementem*, n. 49.) The Apostolical Constitutions, or Canons, are a collection of regulations attributed to the apostles, and supposed to have been compiled by Clement, of Rome, whose name they likewise bear. It is the general opinion, however, that they are spurious, and that Clement had no hand in them. They have no external evidence to support them, not being quoted by any of the Christian writers of the first three centuries. They are also destitute of internal evidence, as they contain many superstitions, profane comparisons, mystical expositions, and ascetic regulations, together with glaring inconsistencies, and much false history, which destroy all claim to apostolical origin. They appeared first in the fourth century, but have been much changed and corrupted since that time. They are divided into eight books, consisting of a great number of rules and precepts, relating to the duties of Christians, and particularly the ceremonies and discipline of the church. Though destitute of apostolical sanction and authority, these Canons are valuable as describing the form, customs, and the ceremonies of the churches, about the year 300. We shall have occasion to quote them again.

Origen,* in his Commentary on the Gos-

---

* Origen (184–254) was at the head of the Catechetical School at Alexandria, and was one of the most eminent of the early Christian writers. He compiled a *Hexapla*,

pel of John (t. viii.), makes the following statement on the subject of baptism: "The washing of water (τὸ ὕδατὸς λουτρὸν) is the symbol of the purification of the soul cleansed of all impurity of sin." In his Commentary on the Gospel of Matthew, he says: "We are, therefore, through this washing (λουτρὸν) buried with Christ in regeneration."

Cyprian,* in his Second Letter to Donatus, calls baptism *lavacrum salutarem*—the salutary bath; also *aquæ salutaris lavacrum*—the bath of salutary water (epist. ii. *Ad Donat.*), and *lavacrum vitale*—vital bath (epist. vii. *Ad Jubaian.*). In his tract, *De Baptismo*, he

---

or Polyglot Bible, and wrote commentaries on Scripture, treatises on the resurrection, martyrdom, prayer, and a defence against Celsus.

* Cyprian (died A. D. 258) was Bishop of Carthage, and an illustrious Father of the African Church. He is the author of some remarkable letters, addresses, and treatises; among these latter may be mentioned the *De Gratia Dei* (On the Grace of God), and *De Idolorum Vanitate* (On the Vanity of Idols).

writes: "Water cleanses indeed the body, but the Holy Ghost sets his seal upon the soul, so that with our bodies washed in clean water, and our hearts purified, we may draw near to God."

Gregory Thaumaturgus,* in his Sermon on Christ's Baptism, speaks of "the immersion of Christ, which took place in the river Jordan."

Lactantius:† "When man, cleansed by the holy washing;" *lavacrum.* (*De Divinis Institutionibus*, lib. viii.)

---

* Gregory Thaumaturgus, so called on account of the number of miracles he is said to have performed during his life and after his death, was Bishop of Neo Cæsarea, and flourished A. D. 245. He composed a panegyrical discourse on Origen, a creed, a paraphrase on Ecclesiastes, and some sermons.

† Lactantius (died A. D. 325) was an eminent Christian writer, and a most elegant Latin writer. He is the author of the remarkable treatise *De Divinis Institutionibus* (On the Divine Institutes), in which he exposes the errors of heathenism and sets forth the truth and excellence of Christianity. He wrote also on the *Death of Persecutors,* and the *Wrath of God.*

Eusebius,* in his Ecclesiastical History (i. c. 10), makes use of the following expression: " That we might be plunged in the bath of baptism . . . . . ." In the succeeding chapter, he alludes to the cleansing of the body and that of the soul.

Cyril † of Jerusalem, in his Discourses to

---

* Eusebius (270–340), Bishop of Cæsarea, in Palestine, was a writer of great learning and vast research, and the father of ecclesiastical history. His chief works are the *Chronicon*, a history of the world down to the year of our Lord 327 and 328; the *Evangelical Preparation*, in fifteen books, a collection of such extracts from the old heathen authors as were fitted to make the mind regard the evidence of Christianity in a favorable light; the *Evangelical Demonstration*, in twenty books, written to convince the Jews of the truth of Christianity; and the *Ecclesiastical History*, in ten books, which extends to the year 324.

† Cyril (315–386), Bishop of Jerusalem, was an eminent church Father, whose writings are exceedingly valuable on account of their theology as well as their vigor, profundity, and beauty. He is well known for his catechetical discourses, of which there are twenty-three still extant. They are divided into two classes; the first eighteen are addressed to catechumens deemed worthy of baptism, and are a brief exposition of the general doctrines of Christianity; the remaining five are addressed to persons already

the catechumens he was preparing for baptism, says to them: "You are about to descend into the baptistery in order to be plunged in water (εἰς τὸ ὕδωρ καταβαίνειν). (*Catech.* iii.) ...... For he who is plunged in water is surrounded on all sides by water; thus the apostles were baptized in the Holy Spirit, but with this difference, however, that whilst the water can reach only the outer surface of the body, the Holy Spirit cleanses in a mysterious manner the inner soul." (*Catech.* xvii.) In his second Mystagogical Lecture, he says: "You have been plunged three times in water, to symbolize by the three immersions the three days our Saviour was buried in the tomb." The discourses of Cyprian give us a minute and very interesting account of the rites of baptism and the Lord's Supper.

---

baptized; they are distinguished by the name of Mystagogical Lectures, and are chiefly devoted to the explanation of the nature of the ordinances.

Epiphanius,* in his Treatise on Heresies, writes: "Instituting the washing (λουτρὸν) of baptism, he (the Saviour) said: 'Go ye, and baptize in the name of the Father, and of the Son, and of the Holy Ghost.'" (*Hæreses*, vii.)

Basil,† in his Sermon *De Baptismo:* "As our Lord Jesus Christ was corporeally buried in the sepulchre three days and three nights, so man, in imitation of this sacred mystery, is by trine immersion buried, and then by emersion resuscitated again."

Augustine, in his Sermon *De Mysterio Baptismatis*, which he addressed to catechumens, who were candidates for baptism, expresses himself in the following manner: "When

---

* Epiphanius (born about A. D. 330) was Bishop of Salamis. Among his writings the most important is his *Panarion*, or Catalogue of All Heresies (eighty in number).

† Basil (329–379), Bishop of Cæsarea, in Cappadocia, is one of the most eminent and eloquent of the Greek Fathers. He was surnamed the Great on account of his learning and piety. He wrote homilies, expositions, panegyrics, a revision of the Septuagint, and letters.

standing in this font before we bathe your whole body (*ante quam vos toto corpore tingueremus*), we have asked: 'Believest thou in God omnipotent our Father? ....' After you have promised to believe, we immerse (*demersimus*) three times your heads (under the water) in the sacred font. For it is right that you should be immersed three times, who receive baptism in the name of the Trinity, and in the name of Jesus Christ, who rose the third day from the dead. This immersion (*demersio*) repeated three times is the symbol of the burial of the Lord; thus you are buried with Christ in baptism, and with Christ resuscitate in the faith, that purified of your sins, and clothed with Christian virtue, you may live in holiness." Here Augustine quotes the words of the apostle Paul in his Epistle to the Romans (c. vi. 3–5).

Juvencus,* a Christian poet of the fourth

---

* Juvencus, a Christian poet, who flourished in the time of Constantine, and wrote a number of poems, all of which

century, paraphrases Matthew iii. 14 in the following manner:

"Shouldst thou not be immersed in water by worthier hands than mine,
Since thy own washing could cleanse me better,
Said John . . . ."
(Historia Evangelica.)

Prudentius,* in his *Psychomachia*, refers to baptism as follows:

---

are lost, except his *Historia Evangelica*. This is an account of our Saviour's life and actions, in four books. It is written in hexameters, and closely adheres to the narrative of the Evangelists. It may be seen in the *Bibliotheca Patrum*.

* Prudentius, a Christian poet of the fourth century, was a native of Spain. His principal works are the *Cathemerinon*, twelve hymns for daily use; the *Apotheosis*, a defence of the doctrine of the Trinity; the *Hamartigeneia*, a work on the origin of evil; the *Psychomachia*, the triumph of the Christian graces in the soul of the believer; *Contra Symmachum*, a polemic against the heathen gods; *Peri Stephanon*, fourteen poems in praise of Spanish and other martyrs; and lastly the *Diptychon*, or forty-eight poems on scriptural incidents and personages. Prudentius has been called the "Horace and Virgil of the Christians."

"Then the immortal tunic, which, with skilful hands,
Holy Faith has woven, and which affords an impenetrable covering,
She herself would give to those who, with their bathed chests, are about to be born again."

Alcuinus Avitus, Archbishop of Vienna (A. D. 481), says, in his hymn *De Diluvio Mundi:*

"Whoever is washed with Christ's baptism is in the Ark."

Leo the Great* writes in his Sixteenth Epistle: "In baptism trine immersion represents the three days' burial (*sepulturam triduam imitatur trina demersio*), and the rising from the waters (*elevatio ab aquis*) is a symbol of the resurrection."

Maximus, Bishop of Turin, says, in one of his Homilies: "*Hic in fonte homo mergitur*"—Here in the font man is immersed.

In his *Historia Ecclesiastica Gentis Anglo-*

---

* Leo the Great was elected Pope of Rome, in 440, and is at the head of the writers of the Latin Church in the fifth century. The most important of his works are his Letters and Sermons, of which there are two volumes.

rum (lib. ii. c. 16), the Venerable Bede gives the following account of the missionary labors of Paulinus:

"King Edwin, with all the nobility of the nation, and a large number of the common sort, received the faith and the washing of regeneration in the eleventh year of his reign, which is the year of the incarnation of our Lord 627...... So great was then the fervor of the faith, and the desire of the washing of salvation among the nation of the Northumbrians, that Paulinus stayed with them thirty-six days, fully occupied in catechising and baptising .... during which days, from morning till night, he did nothing else but instruct the people, resorting from all villages and places, in Christ's saving word, and when instructed he washed them with the water of absolution in the river Glen.* In the Province of Deiri, he baptized

---

* Now called Bowent.

in the river Sarle, which runs by the village of Cataracte,* for as yet oratories or fonts could not be made in the infancy of the Church in those parts."†

The Fourth Council of Toledo, held in A. D. 633, decreed but one immersion, saying that it was not befitting to immerse three times the person baptized (*Non oportere ter mergere eum qui baptizetur*). (Cap. 5.) But both the simple and triple forms of immersion continued to prevail in the Latin churches, whilst the Greek churches persisted in practising trine immersion only, and still hold to it. In the Ordo Romanus, a ritual composed in the eighth century, we find trine immer-

---

* Catterick, in the north riding of York.

† In a plan of Paulinus' second edifice (Edifice of the Metropolitan Church of St. Peter's at York) the probable position of a wooden baptistery, enclosing a spring still remaining, is pointed out. Bede mentions this oratory as being built in haste for the express purpose of baptizing King Edwin. This circumstance would seem to indicate that baptisteries were formerly erected in England.

sion prescribed in the following form: "*Ego te baptizo in nomine Patris, et mergit semel; et Filii, et mergit iterum; et Spiritus Sancti, et mergit tertio.*" I baptize thee in the name of the Father (and immerses once), and of the Son (and immerses a second time), and of the Holy Ghost (and immerses the third time).

Isidore,* in his work *De Offic. Ecclesiast.* (c. 24), says that "in baptism the stains of sin are washed away through the bath of regeneration (*abluuntur per regenerationis lavacrum*);" and adds, "Therefore, when we are baptized in Christ, we are born again of water (*per aquam renascimur*), that being purified we might live."

---

* Isidore, Bishop of Seville, flourished at the beginning of the seventh century. He is among the earliest representatives of the church in Spain, and was one of the most distinguished ecclesiastical writers of his time. His works, bearing on theological, ascetical, liturgical, historical, and philosophical subjects, are very numerous. The Mosarabic Liturgy, which became the text-book of Spanish worship, was principally from his hand.

The Gothic Missal * contains the following form of prayer, which was used at the ceremony of the benediction of the baptismal fonts: "We pray our Lord God that he will sanctify this font, so that all who will descend into this font (*ut omnes qui descenderint in hunc fontem*) may receive through the washing of the most blessed regeneration (*lavacrum beatissimæ regenerationis*) the remission of all their sins."

Bernard,† in his Sermon on the Lord's Supper, says: "Baptism is the first of all the sacraments, in which we are planted to-

---

* This Gothic Missal is from a very old manuscript, the date of which is uncertain. It differs in some respects from the Roman.

† Bernard (died A. D. 1153) was one of the most influential theologians of the middle ages. He was called the *Mellifluous Doctor*, and his writings "a river of paradise." His works are exceedingly numerous. They consist of four hundred and thirty-nine letters, addressed to the leading persons of his time on ecclesiastical and public affairs; of three hundred and forty sermons; and of some devotional and controversial tracts.

gether into the likeness of his (Christ's) death. Hence trine immersion (*trina mersio*) represents the triduum (or three days), which we are about to celebrate." (*In Cœna Domini.*)

Pope Celestine,* in his *Opusculum Octavum*, writes : " Baptism is the washing of the body (*corporis ablutio*), which represents the inner purification of the soul. How great therefore the virtue of water, since it can reach the body, and at the same time cleanse the heart ! "

Thomas Aquinas† makes the following important statement in his *Summa Theologiæ*

---

* Celestine, Pope of Rome, in the thirteenth century.

† Thomas Aquinas, or Thomas of Aquino (1224-1274), is the most remarkable representative of the scholastic theology of the middle ages. His chief works are *A Commentary on the Four Books of Sentences of Peter Lombard*; the *Summa Theologiæ*, which is the first attempt at a complete theological system ; *Quæstiones Disputatæ et Quodlibetales*, and *Opuscula Theologica*. Aquinas was often called by his enthusiastic scholars the " Second Augustine."

(P. iii. qu. 66, art. 7): "The symbol of Christ's burial is more expressively represented by immersion, and for that reason, this mode of baptizing is more common and more commendable." (*In immersione expressius repræsentatur figura sepulturæ Christi, et ideo hic modus baptizandi est communior et laudabilior.*)

As regards the manner in which baptism used to be administered, Tertullian says, that the Christians of his time were immersed by *bowing down* with great simplicity, without pomp, and in a few words. " Quoniam tanta simplicitate, sine pompa, sine apparatu novo aliquo, denique sine sumptu homo in quam *demissus*, et inter pauca verba tinctus." (*De Baptismo*, c. 2.) The meaning of *demisso capite, demisso vultu, demissis oculis*, is familiar to every classical scholar. The primitive mode appears to have been this: The administrator and candidate both standing in the water,* the former placed his right hand on the head of the candidate, and, pronouncing the baptismal words, gently bowed him forward,† till he was completely immersed in the water.‡ In some very ancient paintings, the candidate is represented as standing in the water up to his middle, and the administrator by his side bending him forward. The most remarkable of these paintings is that of the Catacomb of San Ponziano, outside of Rome, in the chapel called "Capella del Battisterio."‖ The Baptism of the Saviour is roughly sketched and painted in the old technical style. The Redeemer is repre-

---

* See Ambrosius, *De Sacrament.*, lib. i. c. 5; and Gregory, *De Sacram.*, lib. *De Sab. Pentecost.*

† This is the meaning of Prudentius, when he speaks of the candidates with their "bathed chests:" *pectoribus lotis.*

‡ Pauli Aringhi, *Roma Subterrannea*, ii. lib. 6. c. 4, *De Baptismo.* Joan Ciampini, *Vetera Monumenta.*

‖ Chapel of the Baptistery, a picture of which forms our frontispiece.

sented up to his waist in clear water, with a nimbed head of regular features, inclosed by long falling hair and a small beard. John stands on a bank to the right, holding a reed, and placing his hand on the Saviour's head. On the left bank an angel, resting upon a cloud, holds the Saviour's garments. At its feet is a stag or deer, looking fixedly at the pure water, symbol of the catechumen ardently desiring the waters of baptism.

Below is painted on the wall a cross set with precious stones, and ornamented with flowers and leaves, and two candlesticks. The cross descends into the water.

The symbols of the Redeemer, A and Ω (Alpha and Omega) are seen suspended from the arms of the cross. Inwoven in this manner these letters formed a frequent symbol in the early church, and were considered as expressive of the supreme divinity of our Saviour, His eternity and immutability, His creative and all-embracing presence and energy. According to Boldetti * these paintings belong to the fifth or sixth century. They will be found reproduced in the large picture we give of the Baptistery of the Catacomb of San Ponziano. (*See Frontispiece.*)

The annexed engraving (Fig. 1.) reproduces a fresco found in the ancient Basilica of St. Clement, at Rome, lately discovered by excavating the soil beneath the modern church of the same name. This painting, which is on the southern wall near the western angle, represents an archbishop, with the Greek pallium, baptizing by immersion a young man of barbaric type. From its vicinity to another painting, alluding to St. Cyril's first mission to the Bulgarians, it probably represents the baptism of the Cham of the Chazari, if not that of Rastices, Duke of Moravia, or Borgoris Michael, Duke of Bohemia, for all these three were converted by St. Cyril and

---

* Boldetti, *Osservazioni sopra i Cimiteri di Santi Martiri ed Antichi Cristiani di Roma.*

Fig. 1.—BAPTISM OF A CONVERT BY CYRIL, MISSIONARY IN BULGARIA.

his brother Methodius.* This fresco is probably of the ninth century.

There is a miniature of the eighth or ninth century, representing the rite of baptism by immersion, which belongs to an unnumbered

---

* "St. Clement and his Basilica in Rome," by Rev. Joseph Mullooby.

manuscript in the large library of the Minerva in Rome. The Redeemer stands in the water up to his waist, John places his right hand upon the Saviour's head, and on the other side of the stream are ministering angels. The title of this valuable manuscript is "Benedictio Fontis," or, Blessing of the Font, represented in the annexed woodcut (Fig. 2.),

Fig. 2.—BENEDICTION OF THE FONT.

in which the archbishop, surrounded by his clergy, pronounces a special blessing upon the baptismal waters, previous to administering the rite. The short figures, the characteristics of this manuscript, are even more reminiscent of the antique than the Terence, No. 3868, which is of the eighth or ninth century, and is now preserved in the Vatican. It contains fourteen miniature paintings on eight parchment leaves.

In the sacristy of the ancient church of San Celso, at Milan, is still preserved an antique diptych, or church book, in which were inscribed the names of the *competentes*, or candidates for baptism. This diptych contains a picture of the Baptism of Christ. In his Memoir of St. Celsus, who was a bishop at Milan, Bugati, a canonical priest, alludes to this picture as follows: "The Redeemer is represented immersed in the water according to the ancient discipline of the church, observed for many centuries in the administration of baptism. John holds in his left hand a curved and knotty staff, and places his right upon the Saviour's head. Finally the Holy Spirit descends from heaven in the form of a dove. This scene is found depicted on the most ancient Christian monuments." * According to Bugati, this picture is of the fifth or sixth century, but the absurd manner in which the water, instead of being level, is raised into a hillock, clearly shows it to be a production of the middle ages.

The great door of the ancient Basilica of St. Paul, outside the walls of Rome, burnt in 1823, and replaced by the modern magnificent Basilica of the same name, was enriched with figures, engraved in outline in the bronze, and filled in with silver. This door had been cast in Constantinople in the eleventh century. The whole front was divided in six equal parts in width, and nine in height, giving fifty-four oblong compartments, containing subjects, figures, and inscriptions. The subjects were taken from

---

* Bugati, *Memoria di San Celso—Appendice.*

the life of Christ, from the annunciation and birth to the ascension, and the coming of the Holy Ghost. In the second square of the first segment on the left hand was a figure of the Baptism of Christ. Our Saviour was represented standing up to his waist in the middle of the river Jordan, his clothes lying by, and John on the bank, with his right hand on the shoulder of Jesus. On the upper part was the word "baptism." This sculpture is faithfully reproduced in the *Storia delle Arte* of Agincourt.

The woodcut (Fig. 3) represents the ceremony of baptism according to the Russian rite. It is taken from a Bulgarian chronicle, a Runic manuscript of the thirteenth or fourteenth century, which is preserved in the library of the Vatican.

In his work on the ancient Christian monuments, Ciampini reproduces a picture of the baptism of Valerian by immersion, taken from an antique fresco, painted by a master

Fig. 3.—CEREMONY OF BAPTISM ACCORDING TO THE RUSSIAN RITE. FROM A RUNIC MANUSCRIPT OF THE 13th OR 14th CENTURY.

of the Greek school established in Italy in the ninth or tenth century. It was still to be seen in Ciampini's time, although partially injured, in the ancient church of St. Andrea, in Barbara, which was built on the ruins of the ancient Basilica Sicimana in the fifth century. It is, however, now quite destroyed.*

The Hotel de Ville of Rheims, in France, contains a large canvas painting of the fif-

---

* Ciampini, *Vetera Monumenta*, t. i. c. 8.

teenth century, representing the baptism of King Clovis by trine immersion.*

Mention might be made of many other ancient paintings of baptism by immersion, but time and space forbid. We will merely, for the present, indicate to our readers the existence of a Greek Monologue, or Calendar, of the ninth or tenth century, and another Greek manuscript, the Book of the Evangelists, of the twelfth century, and manuscript No. 1643, which are all in the library of the Vatican, and in which baptism is represented according to the primitive mode.†
We will again refer to this subject in our description of the various baptisteries of Italy.

The custom of trine immersion, which began as early as the third century, continued till the Reformation. It was prescribed in

---

* *La Moyen Age et la Renaissance*, vol. ii.
† The same subject is found in a miniature painting of *L'Histoire de la Belle Hélène*, a manuscript of the fifteenth century, preserved in the Royal Library of Brussels.

the Prayer Book * of Edward VI. of England, but was afterwards omitted.

Baptism was accompanied in the earlier times of the church with various forms and ceremonies, some of which are still retained in the Greek and Romish churches. These additions to the simplicity of the ordinance began at a very early period. Thus it became customary to exorcise the converts previous to their receiving baptism. This exorcism, which was at first nothing else than calling upon them to renounce the devil and all his works, was subsequently modified so as to include certain prayers, adjurations in the name of Christ, commanding the demon to quit the persons about to be baptized, and imposition of hands. Tertullian, in his Apology (c. xxiii.), and Origen, in his work *Contra Celsus* (lib. vii.), speak of exorcism as of

---

* This Prayer Book was compiled by Cranmer and Ridley, assisted by eleven other divines, and published in 1549.

ordinary occurrence; and the Council of Carthage, in 255, decreed that heretics and schismatics were first to be exorcised with imposition of hands, and then to be baptized before they could be admitted as true members of the Catholic Church. In the passage alluded to above, Tertullian thus speaks of the benefits conferred upon the pagans by exorcism: "Were it not for the Christians, who could rescue your souls and bodies from the power of the hidden enemies that destroy everything? I allude to the demons, who continually beset you, and whom we cast out of you without reward or payment. We might have satisfied our revenge by merely leaving you an undisputed prey to the impure spirits. And you, forgetting the benefit of our protection, prefer to treat as enemies us, who not only do you no harm, but are even necessary to your welfare—we are enemies, it is true, not of men, but of error." Cyril of Jerusalem attached great importance to exorcism, for in one of his Lectures he says: "As mixed metals cannot be purged without fire, so neither can the soul be purged without exorcisms, which are divine, and gathered out of the Scriptures." (*Catech.* xvii.)

Turning to the East, as a symbol of turning to God, was one of the ceremonies connected with baptism in ancient times. When the persons to be baptized entered the baptistery, where they were to make their renunciation of Satan, and their confession of faith, they were placed with their faces towards the West, and commanded to renounce Satan with some gesture or rite; this they did by striking their hands together as a token of abhorrence, by stretching out their hands against him, by exsufflation, and by spitting at him, as if he were present. They were then turned round to the East, and desired to lift up their hands and eyes to heaven, and enter into covenant with Christ, the Sun of Righteousness. "The West," says Cyril,

" is the place of darkness, and Satan is darkness, and his strength is in darkness. For this reason ye symbolically look towards the West when ye renounce that prince of darkness and horrors." (*Catech. Myst.*, ii.) Jerome says: "First we renounce him that is in the West, who dies to us with our sins; and then, turning to the East, we make a covenant with the Sun of Righteousness, and promise to be his servants." (*Comment.*, lib. iii.) Severus Alexandrinus,* referring to this custom, says, in his treatise *De Baptismo:* "He anoints the whole body of him who is to be baptized, and leads him into the baptistery, with his face turned towards the East." (*De Ritibus Baptismi.*)

Insufflation was next added; it consisted in breathing upon the catechumen before baptism, to signify the expulsion of the devil, and again after immersion to symbolize the

---

* Severus, Bishop of Alexandria, flourished A. D. 646. He is the author of several treatises.

gift of the Holy Ghost. Cyril of Jerusalem exhorted his catechumens " to receive exorcism with diligence in the time of catechising; for whether it was insufflation or exorcism it was to be esteemed salutary to the soul." (*Catech.*, xvii.)

Tertullian informs us that it was the custom in his time to give the baptized person a portion of milk and honey, to denote his entrance into the Promised Land of Canaan, and that he belonged to the spiritual Israel. (*De Corona*, lib. xv.) Milk and honey were also given in token of his spiritual youth, and of his reception of spiritual gifts and graces. This custom seems to have been discontinued after a few centuries.

Another addition was made, that of anointing the catechumen with oil before baptism, and with unguent after. This custom is mentioned by Tertullian,[*] Cyprian,[†] Cyril,[‡]

---

[*] *De Baptismo.*
[†] Cyprian, epist. lxiii., *Ad Jubaian.*
[‡] Cyril, *Catech. Mystag.*, ii.

and Chrysostom.* Unction symbolized the gift of the Holy Spirit, and also indicated that the baptized person was ready as a wrestler in the ancient games to fight the good fight of faith. The form in the Liturgy of Edward VI. was: "Almighty God, the Father of our Lord Jesus Christ, who hath regenerated thee by water and the Holy Ghost, and hath given unto thee remission of all thy sins; may he vouchsafe to anoint thee with the unction of his Holy Spirit, and bring thee to the inheritance of everlasting life. Amen." Anointing with oil was retained in the Church of England for a short time after the Reformation. It is still practised in the Church of Rome. The Greek Church anoints the whole body; the Romish the crown of the head only.

After baptism it was customary to wear white garments, in token of the innocence

---

* Chrysostom, *Homilia*, xxii.

of soul, which by this rite the converts were supposed to have acquired.* These garments, which were commonly worn eight days, were metaphorically called the garments of Christ, or the mystical garments. Jerome, writing to Fabiola, alludes to this custom in these words: "We are to be washed with the precepts of God, and when we are prepared for the garment of Christ, putting off our coats of skins, we shall put on the linen garment that hath nothing of death in it, but is all white, that rising out of the waters of baptism, we may gird about our loins with truth, and cover the former filthiness of our breasts."† Gregory the Great, in his *Sacramentarium*, gives the following charge at the delivery of the white robes to the neophytes: "Receive the white and immaculate garment, which thou mayest

---

* Tertullian, *De Resurrectione Carnis*. Cyril of Jerusalem, *Catech.*, xviii.

† Jerome, *Ad Fabiolam*, epist. cxxviii.

bring forth without spot before the tribunal of our Lord Jesus Christ, that thou mayest have eternal life. Amen."

In his account of the baptism by immersion of Cedoaldo, King of the Anglo-Saxons, by Sergius, Pope of Rome, Paulus Warnefridus says:

> "Fonte renascentis quem Christi gracia purgans
> Protinus *Albatum* vexit in arce poli."
> (*De Gestis Lungobard.*, lib. vi. c. 15.)

Venantius Fortunatus * writes in one of his poems:

> "Candidus egreditur nitidis exercitus undis,
> Atque vetus vitium purgat in amne novo
> *Fulgentes animas vestis* quoque candida signat
> Et grege de *niveo* gaudia Pastor habet."

At the baptism of great men many of the attendants clothed themselves also in white. In an epistle of Marcus Gazensis † it is re-

---

* Venantius Fortunatus, Bishop of Poitiers, flourished A. D. 560. He wrote eleven books of poems, and short treatises on the Lord's Prayer, and the Apostles' Creed.

† Marcus, a writer of the fourth century.

corded that, at the magnificent baptism of Theodosius the Younger, a splendid procession accompanied the newly baptized prince from the church to the palace. The leaders on the occasion were clothed in white garments, which made the company look as if it had been covered with snow; and all the senators and men of quality, and soldiers in their ranks carried lamps in their hands, that one would have thought the stars had appeared upon earth.

The white garment was made to fit the body tightly, and was bound round the middle with a girdle-sash; the sleeves were either plain, like those of a cassock, or else full, and gathered close on the wrists, like the sleeves of a shirt. It resembled much the tunic worn by the ancients, and which was called by the Greeks *poderis* (reaching to the feet), and by the Romans *talaris* (reaching to the ankles). It was also designated as the *Alba*, or *Alb*, from its white color.

Candles were lighted after baptism, and placed in the hand of the person baptized, as early as the fourth century, as an emblem of the illumination of the Spirit. This custom is mentioned by Ambrosius in his fifth treatise, *Ad Virg. Laps.*, and is still practised in the Church of Rome.

The kiss of peace, which the neophytes received after baptism, denoted that they were brought into the new spiritual relations of Christian brotherhood and church fellowship. Chrysostom makes allusion to this custom, when, comparing the spiritual with the natural birth, he says: " Here no sufferings, no tears, but greetings, kisses, and embraces of brethren, who acknowledge their new member." (*Sermo.* i.)

In the ancient African Church it was usual to give, with milk and honey at baptism, a portion of bread, seasoned with salt, that the neophyte might have a foretaste, as it were, of the Holy Supper.

The custom of putting a little salt in the mouth of the baptized, to signify the wisdom and taste for heavenly things, which every Christian should have, and that of touching his nostrils and ears with spittle, to denote that his ears are to be ever open to truth, and that he should ever feel the sweet odor of virtue; these two ceremonies were not introduced before the eighth century. They are still retained in the Romish Church.

The washing of the feet of the baptized neophyte used to be practised in some churches.

From a period as early as the second and third centuries, Easter and Pentecost were considered solemn times for the administration of baptism; thus derogating from the apostolic practice, which was to baptize converts whenever opportunity served. Tertullian informs us that baptism was confined, except in cases of urgency, to these two great festivals. (*De Baptismo*, xix.) Easter was celebrated in memory of Christ's death and resurrection, and Pentecost was chosen as the anniversary of the great Jewish feast, when the apostles were baptized with the Holy Ghost and with fire, and they themselves commenced their puplic ministry by baptizing three thousand persons. The rite of baptism was performed on Easter Sunday eve, and Pentecostal eve, that is, on the preceding Saturday evening, when there was a special ceremony of blessing the Font. The neophytes used to wear the white garments (*Alb*) then given them throughout the following week, which obtained from this custom the name of *Septimana in Albis.** The Sun-

---

* Inscriptions have been discovered on some sepulchral slabs, indicating that the deceased had died shortly after receiving baptism, and during the eight days in which the white garments were worn. Thus, " IN ALBIS RECESSIT; ALBAS SUAS OCTABAS PASCHÆ AD SEPULCRUM DEPOSIVIT." "He departed in the albs (that is the white garments) a few days after he had been baptized. He laid at the sepulchre his white garments of Passover." Gregory of Tours, in his History of France (*Epitome*. c. xx.), makes

day following was called *Dominica in Albis depositis*, because those who had been baptized then threw off their white robes, which were laid by in the church as evidence against them if they broke their baptismal vows. Whitsunday (White Sunday), the English name for Pentecost, is supposed to have been so called from the white garments worn by the newly baptized catechumens to whom that ordinance was administered on the vigil of Pentecost.

Epiphany was also one of the stated times for the performance of the rite of baptism in the Greek Church (See Leo the First, epist. xvi.), and in the churches of Africa (Victor of Utica, *De Persecut. Vandal.*, lib. ii.). In the celebration of Epiphany, the Greek Church appears to have dwelt more strongly than the Latin Church upon the baptism of our

---

allusion to the following inscription, which attests the same fact : " IN ALBIS RECESSIT INGOMERES. " " Ingomeres departed in the albs."

Lord, and his manifestation (ἐπιφάνεια) to the world. Hence it is termed by Gregory Nyssenus "ἡ ἡμέρα τῶν φωτῶν"—the day of lights—and by others, "τὰ φῶτα," or "ἅγια φῶτα"—the lights, or holy lights—because baptism itself, as we have already seen, was generally called φῶς and φώτισμα, from the enlightenment it was thought to produce.

With respect to the persons in whom is vested the office of administering baptism, Tertullian says, that it belonged to the bishop (*De Baptismo*, xvii.), although he admits the validity of lay-baptism, when administered by laymen in cases of urgent necessity; so does the Council of Eliberis, A. D. 305, and also Jerome (*Adversus Luciferianos*), who says: "Hence it appears that without permission from the bishop no presbyter nor deacon has the right of baptizing; still if there be absolute necessity, we know, it is allowed to laymen to baptize." Basil, however (epist. i., *Ad Amphil.*), seems to have held the contrary opinion, and the *Apostolical Constitutions* (cap. x., l. iv.) forbid laymen to baptize. Ignatius (epist. *Ad Smyrn.*), and Chrysostom (*De Sacerdotis*, lib. iii.) are also opposed to lay-baptism.

Under the impression that baptism was in itself an actual washing away of all former sins,* there were many persons in the early ages of Christianity, who, though convinced of the truth of the gospel, delayed submitting to the rite till near the close of their lives, hoping thereby to die released from the guilt of sin, and to secure their admission into heaven. This baptism was called *clinic*, from the Greek word κλίνη, a bed; and the persons thus baptized were known as the *clinici*, or clinics. (See Cyprian, epist. lxxvi.) Against this custom the Fathers of the church, Gregory Nyssen,† Gregory Nazian-

---

* Clemens Alexandrinus, *Stromata*, lib. iv. c. 24.

† Gregory Nyssenus: "*Adversus eos qui differunt Baptismum Oratio;*" in his *Opera*, t. ii. p. 222.

zen,* Chrysostom,† Basilius,‡ and others, inveighed in powerful language, and the Council of Neo-Cesarea (A. D. 350), and that of Laodicea (A. D. 363), decreed that no clinic should ever be considered as qualified for ordination to the Christian ministry.

It was customary to administer the Lord's Supper to the neophytes immediately after baptism. In the account which Justin Martyr gives of the celebration of the communion, he says: "After the believer is baptized, and so corporated and made one with us, we lead him to the congregation of the brethren, as we call them, and then with great fervency pour out our souls in common prayers, both for ourselves, for the person baptized, and for all others in the world; that, having embraced the truth, our conversation might be as becomes the gospel, and

---

* Gregory Nazianzen, *Oratio*, xl., c. 28.
† Chrysostom, *Homil.* xxiii., *In Act. Apost.*
‡ Basilius, *Homil. in Baptism.*, c. 3-4.

that we may be found doers of the word, and so at length be saved with an everlasting salvation. Prayers being over, we salute each other with a kiss; after this, bread and a cup of water and wine are brought to the president of the brethren, which he takes, and offers up praise and glory to the Father of all things, through the name of his Son, and the Holy Spirit; and this thanksgiving to God, for rendering us worthy of these his creatures, is a prayer of more then ordinary length. When he has finished the prayers and the thanksgiving, all the people conclude with an audible voice, saying 'Amen.' Now *Amen*, in the Hebrew tongue, is *So be it*. The eucharistic office being thus performed by the president, and concluded with the acclamation of all the people, those whom we call deacons distribute to every one present of this eucharistic bread, and wine and water, and then they carry it to the absent. The food we call the Eucharist, of which none are allowed to be partakers but such only as believe the truths taught by us, and have been baptized in the laver for the remission of sins and to regeneration, and live according to Christ's precepts; for we do not take this as common bread and common drink." (*Apologia*, ii.) It is evident, from this passage of Justin Martyr, that only baptized believers were admitted to the Lord's Supper in the early ages of Christianity. That this was the invariable rule is clearly attested by the form of celebration, contained in the *Apostolical Constitutions* (lib. viii. 12.). It begins thus:

"*The deacon shall say,*

"'Let none of the catechumens, none of the hearers, none of the unbelievers, none of the heterodox stay. Ye who have prayed the former prayer (the prayer for the use of the catechumens) depart. Mothers take away your children. Let no one have aught against any man. Let us stand upright to present unto the Lord our offerings with fear and trembling,'" etc.

Tertullian thus refers to the entrance of the baptized neophyte into the church: "After the declaration of faith has been made, and the pledge of salvation (baptism) received in the name of the Trinity, then follows necessarily a mention of the church; forasmuch as, where the Three are, that is, Father, Son, and Holy Ghost, there is the church, which is their body." (*De Baptismo.*) In his other treatise, *De Corona Militis*, Tertullian speaks of baptism, and then of the Lord's Supper. He says: "We are plunged three times, fulfilling more than our Lord requires in the gospel. Having arisen (from the water), we taste a portion of milk and honey. Then for a whole week we abstain from washing our bodies. We receive the sacrament of the Eucharist in meetings, which are held before daylight."

In his treatise, *De Peccatorum Remissione*,

Augustine, alluding to the Lord's Supper, says that, according to custom, none draw near to it unless they are baptized,* and in his Second Book of *Animadversiones* testifies that the Eucharist was not accustomed to be given to unbaptized persons.†

In the apostolic age, the converts, that is, all who repented of their past sins, and professed to believe in Jesus Christ, were at once baptized and received into the church. But, afterward, this ceased to be the case. None were admitted to baptism, until they had been fully instructed in all the principles of the Christian religion, and had passed through a period of probation. Hence arose the distinction between believers and catechumens. In his *Demonstratio Evangelica*, Eusebius

---

* Augustine: "De sacramento sanctæ mensæ suæ, quò nemo ritè nisi baptizatus accedit." (*De Peccat. Remiss.*, lib. i.)

† " Quia Eucharistia iis dari non solebat, nisi postquam baptizati fuerunt." (*Animadv.*, t. ii.)

speaks of the faithful (πιστοί) and of "those who had not as yet been judged worthy of regeneration through baptism." (Lib. vii. p. 200.) Persons were admitted into the state of catechumens by imposition of hands, prayer, and the sign of the cross, and were called Christians, but were not as yet numbered among the *faithful.* (See Ambrosius, *De Sacrament.*, lib. i., c. 1.) Augustine alludes to this distinction in the following terms: "Ask a man, 'Are you a Christian?' If he be a pagan or a Jew, he will answer, 'I am not a Christian.' But should he say, 'I am a Christian,' then ask him further, 'Are you a catechumen, or one of the faithful?'" (*Tract.* xliv., *In Joan.*, c. ix.) There is, therefore, no pleonasm in the inscription CHRISTIANUS FIDELIS, which is sometimes found on ancient sepulchral slabs, for it indicates that the deceased was a baptized Christian. Augustine speaks of a certain Pontianus as "*Christianus quippe et fidelis,*"* meaning that he had been baptized, and was therefore one of the faithful.

The faithful were in full communion with the church, and had various names, such as "ἀδελφοι"—brethren; "ἅγιοι"—holy; "*electi*"—chosen; "*suscepti*"—received; "*accepti*"—accepted, etc. They were also named "φωτιζόμενοι"—the enlightened; "*illuminati*"—the illuminated, either on account of the knowledge which they had acquired, or again because φωτισμος—enlightenment—was the common name for baptism. Owing to the supposed analogy between baptism and the rites of initiation to the sacred mysteries of the heathen, the faithful were also called "μεμνημένοι," "μυστοί," or "μυσταγώγητοι"—the initiated; in opposition to which the catechumens were designated as "ἀμύητοι," "ἀμυστοι," or "ἀμυσταγώγητοι"—the uninitiated. Oc-

---

* *Confess.*, viii. 6.

casionally the believers were called "τελειοί," or "τελειούμενοι"—the perfect, in allusion to their being qualified for the Lord's Supper, which was mystically denominated "τελετὴ τελετῶν"—the perfection of perfections. The faithful could attend all religious assemblies, while from some the catechumens were summoned to retire. They were permitted to repeat the Lord's Prayer aloud, while the catechumens could only do it in silence. Hence the Lord's Prayer was called "εὐχὴ τῶν πιστῶν" —the prayer of the faithful. The baptized believers were admitted to the Lord's Supper, but the catechumens were excluded.

The catechumens were divided into three classes. 1. The *Audientes*, or Hearers, who were so denominated from their being permitted to hear sermons and the Scriptures read in the church, but who were not allowed to stay and participate in the prayers.* The

---

* Tertullian, *De Pœnitentia.* Cyprian, epist. xiii.

sixth book of the *Apostolic Constitutions* prescribed to the deacon to give them notice to depart, as soon as the bishop had ended his sermon, in the following terms: "*Ne quis audientium, ne quis infidelium*"—no more hearers, no more unbelievers; and then he was to call upon the other catechumens and the faithful to pray for them: "*Orate, catechumeni, et omnes fideles, pro illis cum attentione orent.*" The Audientes usually assembled in the Narthex, or ante-temple. Augustine's treatise *De Catechizandis Rudibus*, was especially designated for this class of catechumens; it was written for the use of the deacon Deogratias, who had under his charge the Audientes of Carthage. The second class of catechumens were designated under the name of *Genuflectentes*, or Kneelers, because they received the bishop's benediction on their knees. A great part of the liturgy particularly applied to this class; it was called " κατηχουμένων εὐχή "—the prayer of the catechumens, and came immediately after the bishop's sermon. (*Apostolical Constitutions*, lib. vi.) They continued in this class for three, and occasionally for seven years.

The third and last class was called by the Greeks βαπτίζομενοι and φωτίζομενοι, and by the Latins *Competentes* and *Electi*, which words, among the ancients, denoted the immediate candidates for baptism, who had delivered their names to the bishop, signifying their intention to be baptized at the next approaching festival of Easter, or of Pentecost. From their petitioning for this favor they were termed *Competentes* * (petitioning together), and from the bishop's approbation or choice, they were styled *Electi*.† Cyril of Jerusalem, in his third Catechetical Lecture, terms this class "φωτίζομενοι," or illuminated, as having received the illumination of catechetical in-

---

* Augustine, *Sermo De Baptismo*.
† See Leo the Great, epist. xvi., *Ad Episc. Silic.*; and also Siricius, epist. i., c. 2., n. 3.

struction, and the author of the *Apostolical Constitutions* uses the word "βαπτιζομενοι," not for those who were already actually baptized, but for those who were desirous of receiving that rite. The Competentes were required to give their names, which were registered in the diptychs, or church books.* Augustine, in his Hundred and thirty-second Sermon, says: "*Ecce Pascha est, da nomen ad baptismum*"—here is Passover, give thy name for baptism. In his Sermon addressed to those who deferred being baptized, Gregory Nyssenus invites them in the following terms: "Give me your names, that I may inscribe them in the books. . . . . . . God will write them on tables which cannot be destroyed." A special form of prayer was offered for the candidates; it will be found in the *Apostolical Constitutions* (lib. viii., c. 7, 8), as follows: "Those who are about to be de-

---

* See Socrates, *Hist. Eccles.*, vii. 21.

dicated to God through Christ shall here bow themselves, and receive the blessing of the bishop in these words: 'O thou, who by the holy prophets hath said to those who are about to dedicate themselves to thee: Wash you, make you clean; and who hast appointed a spiritual regeneration through Christ, look now, we beseech thee, upon these persons soon to be baptized; bless them, sanctify them, and make them worthy to partake of thy spiritual gifts, the true adoption, thy spiritual mysteries, and to be received into the body of the redeemed, through Christ our Saviour, through whom be unto thee all glory, honour, and worship, in the Holy Ghost, for ever. Amen.' Then shall the deacon say: 'Depart, ye candidates for baptism.'"

Previously to their reception of the rite of baptism, the catechumens were repeatedly examined concerning the proficiency they had made in Christian doctrine. They were all exercised for twenty days (Cyril, *Catech.* i.), during which they were obliged to frequent fastings,* prayers, confession of their former sins, which confession was sometimes public and sometimes private, as the wisdom of the church directed.† At this time, the Competentes were taught to repeat the creed, which they were obliged to say before the bishop at their examination for baptism. ‡ With the creed they were also taught to make the proper responses in baptism, particularly the form of renouncing the devil and covenanting with Christ. (Jerome, *Adv. Luciferan.*) Some days before baptism they went veiled, or with their faces covered, in order that their mind might be more at liberty, and

---

* *Apostolical Constitutions*, vii., c. 23; Tertullian, *De Baptismo*, xx.; Jerome, epist. *Ad Pammach.*; Augustine, *De Fide et Oper.*, v. 8.

† Tertullian, *De Pallio;* Eusebius, *In Vita Constantini*, iv. 61; Gregory of Nazianzen, *Serm. in Sacr. Lavacr.*

‡ Cyril, *Catech. Mystag.*, ii.

that the wandering of their eyes might not distract their soul.

With respect to the instruction of the catechumens, it does not appear that any distinct order of ministers officiated as catechists, but that it was only a particular employment, which might devolve on any officer of the church, and which we find, at different times, attached to all the orders of the ministry. Thus this office was sometimes discharged by the bishop himself, especially on Palm-Sunday, on which day, after the sermon, he would take the catechumens apart and explain to them the creed. (Ambrosius, epist. 33; Theodorus,* *Lector Collectam.*, lib. ii.) The presbyters and deacons were also entrusted with this office. In some cases it was confided to a reader, who was called for that reason *Doctor Audientium—*

---

* Theodorus, Bishop of Mopsuestia, in Cilicia, flourished A. D. 392. He wrote commentaries, of which only a few fragments remain.

teacher of the Audientes. (Cyprian, epist. xxiv.) It was no doubt to avoid scandal and suspicion, that the female catechumens were generally taught by that ancient order, the Deaconesses. In the East, where the strict separation between male and female society was then, as now, proverbial, this measure was quite indispensable. The duties of a deaconess consisted in the instruction of female catechumens, and assisting at their baptism;* in visiting sick persons of their own sex; and in performing all those offices, which could not with propriety be exercised by the deacons themselves. The African churches, in a decree of the Council of Carthage, specify among the qualifications of a deaconess, "*ut possit apto et sano sermone docere imperitas et rusticas mulieres, etc.*"—that she be able to teach with suitable and sound doctrine the ignorant and rude women.

---

* Chrysostom, epist. *Ad Innoc.*, pp.

It was the office of the catechists to prepare the candidates for baptism by a course of instruction suited to each, but in what their teaching generally consisted at first, we know no further than that the sum and substance of it was repentance and faith. Such was in fact the character of the teaching of the apostles and others to an unconverted audience. In Paul's addresses to the Jews at Jerusalem, and to the Gentiles at Athens and Rome, his teaching approaches nearest to catechetical instruction. This method was subsequently adopted by the Fathers of the church, who usually began their discourses with the doctrines of repentance and remission of sins, the necessity of good works, and the nature and use of baptism. Then followed in the second and third centuries, an explanation of the so-called Apostles' Creed, which, as we have already said, was always used before the administration of baptism, when the catechumen made an open confession of his faith;* hence the creed was called "Μάθημα," or the *lesson*, because catechumens were obliged to learn it. To the explanation of the creed, some Fathers added that of the nature and immortality of the soul, and an account of the canonical books of Scripture. No mention, however, was made of the Lord's Supper, because, as our readers already know, it was not given to catechumens until after baptism.

The catechists, merely as such, were not allowed at first to instruct their catechumens in the church, but only in private auditories appointed for that purpose. That there were such catechetical schools in many places is evident from the Sixty-seventh Novella of the Emperor Leo,† who calls them " Κατηχού-

---

* Tertullian, *Adversus Praxeas;* Cyprian, epist. lxx.; Cyril of Jerusalem, *Catech. Mystag.* ii.; and Jerome, *Adversus Luceferianos.*

† Leo, surnamed the "Isaurian," was Emperor of Constantinople; died A. D. 741. He wrote a few treatises, which were called *Novellæ*, or "New Works."

μενια," and says that they were a kind of buildings attached to the church. Subsequently, the catechumens received their religious education and training in a portion of the church expressly reserved for that object,* or in a hall adjoining the baptistery. Thus the large room attached to the Baptistery of Constantine in Rome, and now designated by the name of *Oratory of St. Venantius*, was formerly used for the instruction of catechumens, and is still employed for teaching the Romish catechism to children. In the Catacombs of Rome there still exist *cubiculi*, or sepulchral chapels, which contain several graves, and in the angles are seats cut in the rock. There have been found two of these chapels in the Catacombs of St.

---

* Anciently the inner parts of the portico of churches were divided into small places of retirement, sometimes called *cubiculi*, or small chambers, where worshippers might retire for meditation and prayer. They were regarded as a portion of the *catechumenia*, or belonging to the catechumens.

Agnese, which are supposed to have served as places of meeting for catechumens, the seats being for the instructing bishop or deacon. One of these, the larger, was for male catechumens, and the other, on the opposite side, for females. In a cubiculum of the Catacomb of St. Callixtus, there is a low seat or bench, with two higher ones, destined probably for catechumens and their instructors.

As no limit was fixed for the period during which persons were to continue in the state of catechumens, the practice varied at different times. During the apostolic age, catechising and baptizing accompanied one another; but afterwards some interval was thought advisable, the duration of which varied according to circumstances, and to the diligence and zeal of the catechumens themselves. In cases of desperate sickness they were allowed clinic baptism; with the exception, however, of extreme cases, a considerable time was judged necessary, not only to make trial of their conversion, but also to instruct them fully in the principles of the Christian religion. By the Forty-second Canon of the Council of Eliberis, the duration of the catechumenate was limited to two years, on condition, however, that the candidates had led irreproachable lives. ("*Si bonæ fuerint conversationis.*") The Emperor Justinian* required also a probation of two years for the Jews embracing Christianity. Three years are indicated by the *Apostolical Constitutions;* but the Council of Agde (A. D. 506) decreed that a probation of eight months was sufficient. This rule was not rigidly

---

* Justinian (A. D. 483-565) was a Roman emperor, who gained great renown as a legislator. He compiled a code, which comprised all the constitutions of his predecessors, and which is known as the Justinian Code. He harmonized and published, under the title of *Digesta Pandecta*, the authoritative commentaries of the jurists. His *Institutes* is a systematic treatise on the laws, for the guidance of students and lawyers.

adhered to, for we read in the account Socrates* gives us of the conversion of the ancient Burgundians, that they were catechized and baptized in the course of eight days.

---

* Socrates, a celebrated church historian of the fifth century.

PART II.

THE BAPTISTERIES OF ITALY.

IN the times of the apostles and their immediate successors, the converts were baptized in a river, a lake, a sea, and wherever water in sufficient quantity could be found for the administration of the rite by immersion. Thus John the Baptist immersed in the river Jordan at Enon, where there was much water. The Ethiopian Eunuch went down into water lying by the roadside to receive baptism at the hands of Philip. It is not unlikely that Paul baptized Lydia and her household in the river that runs by the city of Philippi. In his Second Apology, Justin Martyr states that this was the custom in his time, and

Tertullian (*De Baptismo*, c. iv.) says that "it makes no difference whether one is baptized in a sea or in a pool, in a river or in a fountain, in a lake or in a bath; nor is there any difference between those whom John immersed in the Jordan, and those whom Peter dipped in the Tiber." Walafrid Strabon acknowledges that the believers in the times of the apostles were baptized with great simplicity in rivers or fountains.* The same admission is made by Honorius Augustus, in his *Gemma Animæ* (lib. iii., c. 106).† We have already seen that Paulinus baptized the Northumbrian converts in the rivers Glen and Sarle in the North of England. In the

---

* "Sciendum autem, primo simpliciter in fluvio vel fontibus baptizatos credentes; ipse enim Dominus noster Jesus Christus, ut in nobis idem consecraret lavacrum, in Jordane baptizatus est à Joanne, et sicut alibi legitur; erat Joannes baptizans in Ænon, juxta Salino, quia aquæ multæ erant." (*De Ritibus Eccles.*, c. 26.)

† "Sciendum est, quòd apostoli, et eorum discipuli in fluvio, vel stagnio, vel in fontibus baptizabant."

Acts of Apollinarius and Victor, it is mentioned that these two missionaries led their catechumens to the sea to administer to them the rite of baptism.*

During the dark days of imperial persecutions the primitive Christians of Rome found a ready refuge in the Catacombs, where they constructed baptisteries for the administration of the rite by immersion. The most remarkable of these is the baptistery in the Catacomb of San Ponziano, on the right side of the Via Ostiensis, and at a short distance beyond the modern Porta Portese. Through this cemetery a stream of water runs, the channel of which is diverted into a reservoir, which was used for administering baptism by immersion from the first to the fourth centuries. A perspective view of this antique baptistery will be found in the Frontispiece. On the arch over the reservoir is a fresco

---

* Martene, *De Antiq. Eccles. Ritib.*, i., p. 3.

painting of the baptism of Christ, which belongs, according to Boldetti,* to the sixth century. In his work, *Roma Sotterranea*,† Bottari gives the following explanation of this painting. He says: "Upon the wall, over the arch, the Redeemer is represented up to his waist in the waters of the river Jordan, and upon his head rests the right hand of John the Baptist, standing on the shore. It is by mistake that modern artists represent Christ in the Jordan up to his knees only, and John pouring water upon his head. And although on the portico of the church of San Lorenzo, outside of the walls of Rome, that saint is seen in a painting pouring water upon the head of San Romano, this was certainly not the case, as this picture is far more modern than those of the first centuries, and the artist was evi-

---

* Boldetti, *Osservazioni sopra i Cimiteri de' Santi Martiri ed Antichi Cristiani di Roma.*

† Bottari, *Roma Sotterranea*, t. i., p. 194.

dently ignorant or wrongly informed concerning the acts of San Lorenzo. It is not improbable, however, that subsequently it became customary to pour water upon the head of the catechumen after he had been immersed.

"On the other shore an angel is seen upon a cloud, holding the Saviour's robe; the Holy Ghost descends like a dove and alights upon the Redeemer. John places his hand upon the head of Christ to immerse him. A hart is also seen standing on the shore and looking fixedly at the water; symbol of the catechumen ardently desiring the waters of baptism, according as Jerome says in his commentary on the Forty-second Psalm: 'He wishes to come to Christ in whom is the source of light, that, being washed by baptism, he may receive the gift of the remission of sins.'"

Behind the reservoir is painted on the wall a cross set with precious stones and ornamented with flowers and leaves, and two candlesticks. The symbols of the Redeemer, A and Ω (Alpha and Omega) are seen suspended from the arms of the cross. Inwoven in this manner, these letters formed a frequent symbol of the early church, and were considered as expressive of the supreme divinity of our Saviour, his eternity and immutability, his creative and all-embracing presence and energy.

The Catacombs of the Vatican and St. Alexander contained natural springs, those of St. Priscilla and St. Callixtus received water by means of canals into cisterns, vestiges of which still remain.

It was only after the conversion of the Emperor Constantine to Christianity that its rites were permitted to be celebrated in public. Under his reign, churches were erected with great splendor. In addition to the basilica itself, it was necessary to have a building in which the baptism of the people who were converted to the gospel might be administered. This rite being performed by immersion, and the number of persons being considerable, because in general it took place only at the two most solemn festivals of the year, a spacious building for this purpose was required, and one was usually erected in the vicinity of a church. The baptistery of Constantine at Rome is the earliest example of this species of building.

The word "baptistery" is derived from the Greek βαπτιστήριον, a large vase, labrum, or piscina of the frigidarium in the ancient Roman baths, which was used to bathe in. It was called by the Romans *baptisicrium*. Pliny mentions a large baptistery he had in his house.* The Christian baptisteries were circular or octagonal in form. The oldest were circular, copied, as some archæologists think, from the circular Roman temples, which

---

* Pliny, lib. ii., epist. 17, and lib. v., epist. 6.

supplied a graceful model for buildings that were not to be so large as churches. It is more probable, however, that the form of these buildings was imitated from some apartment in a Roman bath, most likely the frigidarium, or cold bath, a round hall, a plan of which is shown in the annexed engravings. (Fig. 4.) They represent the frigidarium of the Pompeii baths, discovered some years ago. It is a round chamber, with a ceiling in the form of a truncated cone; near the top is a window, from which it is lighted.

Fig. 4.—SECTION OF FRIGIDARIUM OF BATH, POMPEII.

The plinth, or base of the wall, is entirely of marble, and four niches are disposed round the room at equal distances, with seats for the convenience of the bathers. The alveus, or basin, is twelve feet and ten inches in diameter, three feet deep, and entirely lined with white marble, two marble steps facilitate the descent into the basin. (Fig. 5.) The water ran into this bath in a copious stream, through a spout placed in the wall, three feet and seven inches from the edge of the basin. At the bottom of the alveus is a small outlet for the purpose of emptying and cleansing it. This frigidarium had been highly decorated, and is still remarkable for its preservation and beauty.*

Fig. 5.—PLAN OF FRIGIDARIUM OF BATH, POMPEII.

The internal arrangement of the ancient baptisteries strictly corresponds with the above plan.† They are in most cases circular buildings, surmounted with a dome or cupola. In the centre is a large basin, which

---

* Encyclopædia, article *Bath*.

† The baptistery at Nocera, now known as the Church of Santa Maria Maggiore, was formerly a Roman bath.

was called by the Latins *baptisterium, lavacrum*, and *natatoria*, and by the Greek ecclesiastical writers "κολυμβήθρα," or pool. Socrates, in his Church History (vii. 17), expressly distinguishes the font, or basin, from the baptistery, or the outer building, with which it has sometimes been confounded, and perhaps latterly become synonymous, as "the pool of the baptistery" (κολυμβήθραν τοῦ βαπτιστηρίου). The baptisteries are usually situated in the approach to the western, or principal gate of the church, to typify the initiation of the new Christian. They were generally constructed of large size, in order to afford accommodation to the great number of persons baptized at the three principal festivals of Easter, Pentecost, and Epiphany, and for this additional reason, that as the right of baptizing was reserved only to the bishop, however numerous might be the churches in the larger cities of Italy, still there was but one general baptistery to which all resorted, and which was attached to the Metropolitan or Bishop's Church.

We now give a full list of the baptisteries in Italy, with indication of their form and the time of their foundation.*

BAPTISTERIES.	FORM.	EPOCH OF CONSTRUCTION.
Rome, St. John of Lateran	Octagonal,	4th Century.
" S. Costanza	Circular,	"
Naples, S. Stefania	"	"
Nocera, S. Maria Maggiore	"	"
Milan, S. Giovanni, for men	Octagonal,	"
Milan, S. Stefano, for women	"	"
Pesaro	"	"
Roma, Basilica S. Stefano	"	About A. D. 440.
Classe, Della Petriana	Square,	"
Ravenna, S. Giovanni	"	"
" S. Maria in Cosmedin	"	A. D. 550.
Canosa, in Apulia	Twelve-sided,	6th century.
Triesta, in Istria	Octagonal,	"
Parenzo, "	"	"
Pirano, "	"	"
Cittanova, "	"	"
Capodistria, "	Circular,	"
Aquileja	Octagonal,	"

* See *Il Battistero di Parma da Michaele Lopez*, pp. 124, 125.

BAPTISM AND BAPTISTERIES. 111

BAPTISTERIES.	FORM.	EPOCH OF CONSTRUCTION.
Grado................................	Octagonal,	6th century.
Brescia..............................	Circular,	End of 6th cent.
Novara..............................	Octagonal,	"
Asti..................................	Polygonal,	"
Baveno, on Lake Maggiore.........................	Circular,	6th or 7th cent.
Como................................	Octagonal,	"
Lenno, on Lake Como...	"	"
Gravedona, " " ...	"	"
Menaggio, " " ...	"	"
S. Giovanni in Atrio, on Lake Como................	"	"
Galliano, Prov. of Como.	Irregular,	"
Arsago, Prov. of Milan...	"	"
Berzanò, " " " ...	Octagonal,	?
Mazzo, Prov. of Valtellina	"	?
Castrocaro, near Forli......	Circular,	?
Florence............................	Octagonal,	7th century.
Lucca................................	Square,	"
Bologna............................	Twelve-sided,	"
Serravalle..........................	Octagonal,	8th century?
Pavia, for men................	"	8th century.
" for women............	?	"
Verona..............................	Octagonal,	"
Cividale, in Venetian Provinces........................	"	"
Pola, in Istria...................	Greek Cross,	?
Ascoli...............................	Square,	9th or 10th cent.
Volterra............................	Octagonal,	"
Biella, in Piedmont.........	Greek Cross,	"
Chieri, "	Octagonal,	"
Agliate, Prov. of Milan...	"	"
Mariano, Prov. of Como..	"	"
Varese, " " " ..	"	"
Cremona...........................	"	A. D. 900?

BAPTISTERIES.	FORM.	EPOCH OF CONSTRUCTION.
Dorno, Prov. of Como...	?	11th century.
Castel-Seprio, " ...	Hexagonal,	"
Oggiono, " ...	Octagonal,	"
Abiasca, Diocese of Milan	?	?
Faido, " " "	?	?
Torcello..................	Octagonal,	A. D. 1009.
Murano	"	11th century.
Chioggia	Circular,	"
Rovigno (Istria).........	Heptagonal,	9th century.
Padua.....................	Square,	11th or 12th cent.
Vigolo Marchese, Prov. of Piacenza............	Circular,	"
Genoa, S. Giovanni......	Octagonal ?	?
Reggio, in Emilia.........	?	?
Pisa, " "	Circular,	A. D. 1153.
Parma, " "	Octagonal,	A. D. 1196.
Pistoia.....................	"	A. D. 1337.

BAPTISTERY OF CONSTANTINE.

We may now proceed to speak of this baptistery, which has been ascribed to Constantine, and in which some antiquarians have been willing to discover the remains of *thermæ*, or baths, originally within the precincts of the imperial palace. This building stands at a short distance from the church of St. John of Lateran, and now bears the name of San Giovanni in Fonte, an appellation usually given to the baptisteries in the peninsula. All this region was originally occupied by the house and gardens of a wealthy Roman, Plautius Lateranus, who was put to death by Nero.* The house, subsequently, became one of the imperial palaces. Constantine possessed it in his turn, until he left Rome for his new capital in the East.

That the baptistery cannot be justly entitled to the name it bears, is sufficiently evident from the well-attested fact that Constantine, though he declared himself a Christian, postponed the rite, which was then believed to wash away the stain of every sin, till he found his end approaching, and then was baptized, not at Rome, but at Nicodemia. In fact, this baptistery was not constructed till the pontificate of Sixtus III.,

---

* Rasponus, *De Basilica Laterensis*.
10*

who died in A. D. 440. Anastasius* says that it was he who placed the eight porphyry columns, which decorate the interior of the building. The probability is that these columns had been the ornament of some palatial mansion, a nymphæum, or baths, in the gardens of Lateranus; that Sixtus, wishing to construct a baptistery in connection with the church of St. John, availed himself of these precious materials, and that the baptistery derived its name from the palace in which Constantine had once resided. In 1153, Anastasius IV. raised the walls of the building, and covered it with a new roof.† He must have added the second tier of smaller pillars, which support the attic. Other popes, at different times, contributed additional embellishments. Gregory XIII., in 1572, added the panelled ceiling. Urban VIII., in 1628, and Innocent X., in 1644, en-

---

* Anastasius, *In Vita Sexti* III.
† Ciampini, *De Sacris Ædificiis*, cap. 3.

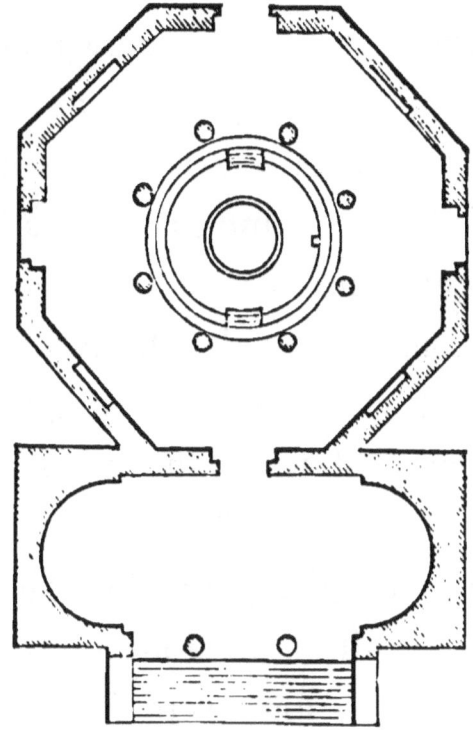

Fig. 6.—PLAN OF BAPTISTERY OF CONSTANTINE.

riched the ceiling and the walls with frescoes by the best masters. A chapel opens out of each side of the baptistery; the one dedicated to John the Baptist, the other to John the Evangelist.*

In the centre of the building is a magnificent circular basin, three feet deep, lined and

---

* Knight, *Architecture in Italy.*

paved with marble. It occupies a large proportion of the building, being about twenty-five feet in diameter. Anastasius, in his Life of Pope Sylvester,* and Damascus,† describe the basin existing in their time as being of porphyry, and covered entirely both within and without with silver, the weight of which was estimated at three thousand and eight pounds. In the middle of the basin stood a column of porphyry, bearing on its top a golden phial full of precious ointment. On the edge of the font were figures of seven harts of solid silver, and a lamb in massive gold, which poured water into the basin, previous to the administration of baptism. This magnificence is in harmony with the descriptions given of the baths in Rome, at the time of Agrippa and the emperors after Augustus, which were built and finished in a style of luxury almost incredible. In his

---

* Anastasius, *In Vita S. Sylvestri.*
† Damascus, *In Pontific. de Sylvest. Pap.*

Eighty-sixth Epistle, Seneca, who inveighs against this luxury, observes that "a person was held to be poor and sordid, whose baths did not shine with a profusion of the most precious materials, the marbles of Egypt inlaid with those of Numidia; unless the walls were laboriously stuccoed in imitation of painting; unless the chambers were covered with glass, the basins with rare Thasian stone, and the water conveyed with silver pipes." These were the luxuries of plebeian baths. Those of the freedmen and the nobility had "a profusion of statues, a number of columns supporting nothing, placed as an ornament merely on account of the expense; the water murmuring down the steps; and the floor of precious stones." (Epist. lxxxvi.) These baths of which Seneca speaks were private baths.*

Though the Baptistery of the Lateran has not on the whole that appearance of an-

---

* Encyclopædia, Article *Bath*.

tiquity, which one might ascribe to a building of the fourth century, still it is certain that the exterior and the general arrangement of the interior have been preserved from the beginning, as may be seen from an ancient design of the building in the baptistery itself, bearing the following inscription: "BAPTISTERIUM RESTITUIT."

A descent of three steps leads to the bottom of the basin, which is provided with a small outlet, which was used for the purpose of emptying it after the ceremony of baptism by immersion had been performed. That this basin was formerly used for the administration of the rite according to the primitive method is evident from the following inscription in Latin verses upon the architrave supported by the columns of porphyry which surround the basin:

GENS SACRANDA POLIS HIC SEMINE NASCITVR ALMO
  QVAM FECVNDATIS SPIRITVS EDIT AQVIS
MERGERE PECCATOR SACRO PVRGANTE FLVENTO
  QVEM VETEREM ACCIPIET PROFERET VNDA NOVVM . . .

In the centre of the basin now stands a modern font, raised on steps of marble, and composed of an antique urn in porphyry, which serves to contain the holy water used in sprinkling infants.

BAPTISTERY OF S. COSTANZA.

Beyond the Porta Pia, near the church of S. Agnese, is a circular building erected by Constantine as a baptistery, and in which the two Constantias, his sister and daughter, are supposed to have been baptized. This baptistery is about eighty feet in diameter; the interior is adorned by a double range of columns supporting arches, on which rises the drum, or circular part, supporting the dome, which is pierced with a clerestory of twelve windows. In the square niche opposite the entrance stood a sarcophagus of porphyry, belonging to the family of Constantine, and which has been removed to the museum of the Vatican. (Fig. 7.)

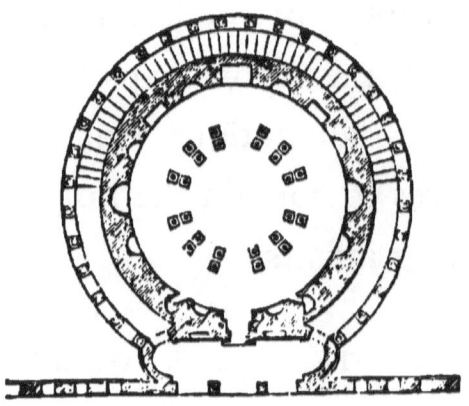

Fig. 7.—PLAN OF BAPTISTERY OF S. COSTANZA, ROME.

Some persons have imagined that this building was neither the work of Constantine, nor, originally, a Christian fabric. They admit that it was the burial place of Constantia and Helena, the daughter of Constantine, because they are unable to account in any other way for the sarcophagus of porphyry found within its walls. But they assert that it was an ancient temple of Bacchus, transferred to a new destination by Constantine or his sons. This opinion is principally founded on the mosaics with which the ceiling of the aisles is adorned, and which represent vine-leaves, bunches of grapes, and different operations of the vintage. But, in the first place, the vine is a Christian emblem,* and was so frequently introduced in the decoration of Christian places of worship, that little weight can be attached to this circumstance. In the second place, it was not till the time of Theodosius that the heathen temples were invaded. It would not have been safe for Constantine to have disturbed the deities that were still revered by so large a proportion of his subjects. In the third place, the architecture of this building is in conformity with the style of the time of Constantine, and does not agree with that of a much earlier date.

We find that Anastasius, in his Life of St. Sylvester, says that Constantine built a bap-

---

* Several tombs and sepulchral chapels in the catacombs are decorated with figures of vines and grapes, emblematical of Christ and his church. See Bottari, plate lxxiv.

tistery close to the church of St. Agnes.* On the other hand, Ammianus Marcellinus says that Constantia and Helena were buried in exactly this situation; and finally, as we have already said, the porphyry sarcophagus was discovered within the walls of this building. From this fact, coupled with the testimony of the historians, it cannot be doubted that this building was eventually used as a sepulchral chapel, but as it is so distinctly stated that Constantine built a baptistery in this situation, and as there are no vestiges of any other buildings, the probability is that the baptistery and the sepulchral chapel are one and the same. It might be built for one purpose, and afterwards used for another, in the case of persons of such consideration as the sister and daughter of Constantine, and

---

* Eodem tempore fecit basilicam S. Martyris Agnetis ex rogatu Constantiæ filiæ suæ, et baptisterium in eodem loco ubi et baptizata est soror ejus Constantia cum filia Augustia Sylvestro episcopo. (Anastasius, *Vita S. Sylvestri.*)

it was in accordance with the custom of those times that they should be buried in the immediate vicinity of holy ground, as was, for example, the cemetery in which the remains of St. Agnes and other martyrs had been discovered. In 1254, the building was converted into a church by Pope Alexander IV., and was then dedicated to another Constantia, who is believed to have founded or rebuilt the adjacent church of St. Agnes.*

BAPTISTERY OF NOCERA DEI PAGANI.

At Nocera dei Pagani, on the railroad from Naples to Castellamare, is a very interesting church, named Santa Maria Maggiore, which was formerly a Roman bath, restored and employed as a baptistery in the fourth century. It is very similar in plan and general arrangement to the baptistery of Constanza at Rome, though somewhat

---

* Knight, *Church Architecture of Italy.*

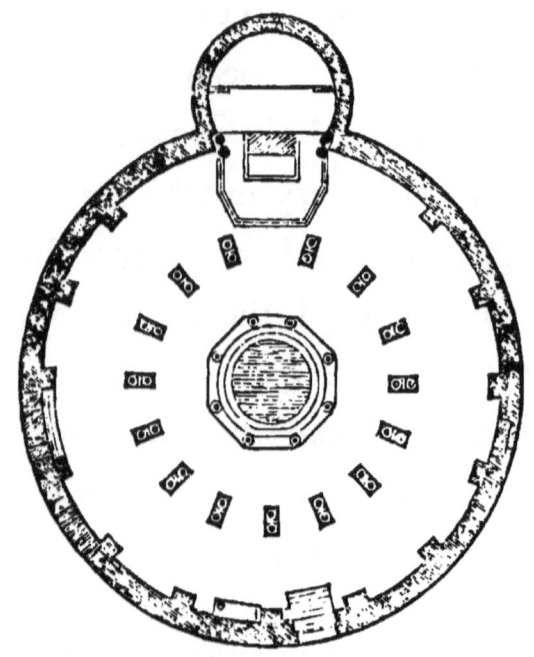

Fig. 8.—PLAN OF BAPTISTERY AT NOCERA DEI PAGANI.

larger, being more than eighty feet in diameter. (Fig. 8.) Its arched roof is supported by a double row of twenty-eight columns of different orders and lengths, of which five are of oriental alabaster, and the rest mostly of ancient marbles. In the centre is a large basin, circular in the interior, and octagonal externally. A descent of three steps leads to the bottom of the basin, which bears a strong resemblance to that of the baths of Pompeii, and was evidently used for the administration of baptism by immersion.* This baptistery is certainly one of the most valuable monuments of antiquity, and is well worth a visit from all who are interested in the study of Christian archæology.

BAPTISTERIES OF MILAN.

In a letter to his sister Marcellina, the celebrated Archbishop of Milan, Ambrosius, refers to the baptisteries, which existed in that city in his time.† One of these is attached to the southern wall of the church

---

* Agincourt, *Storia dell' Arte*, tav. 8, Nos. 9, 10, *Archit.* Isabelle, *Edifices Circulaires*, p. 87, pl. 39. Ricci, *Storia dell' Architettura in Italia*, t. i., p. 158.

† " Octachorum sanctos templum surrexit in usus,
  Octogonus fons est munere dignus eo :
  Hoc numero decuit sacri baptismatis aulam
  Surgere ; quo populo vera salus rediit."
  (Ambrosius.)

of San Lorenzo, is about forty-five feet in diameter, and is approached by a vestibule in the same manner as that of Constantine at Rome, and as in the tomb of his daughter Constantia. This baptistery, now known under the name of San Giovanni alle Fonti, was exclusively used for the baptism of men, and it was here that St. Augustine was buried with Christ in baptism. This baptistery was much injured by the invasion of the Goths, but was restored by Lorenzo, Bishop of Milan, about the end of the fifth century. Another baptistery for the women, erected on the opposite side of the church, was designated under the name of San Stefano alle Fonti. Eunodius, speaking of this baptistery in his Epigrams,* says that it was reconstructed by Eustorgius II., Bishop of Milan, who provided it with a hydraulic contrivance, by means of which the water was

---

* Lib. ii., *Carm. Epigr.* 149.

made to descend from above the font in the form of rain, and fill the large basin previously to the administration of baptism. These two baptisteries still existed in their original form at the beginning of the twelfth century, and are mentioned by Beroldus,* who wrote about the year 1130. Since then very great changes have been made, and they have been so painfully altered, that little remains to attract the attention of the archæologist besides the bare plan of the buildings.

In the magnificent Cathedral of Milan, there is a modern baptistery, a small square temple supported by four columns of marble. It contains an ancient *labrum*, now used as a font, and taken from a bath of the Lower Empire, the rite of baptism by immersion being required by the Ambrosian ritual.

---

* *Ordo Cerim. Eccl. Ambr. Med.*, *De Vigilia Nat. Dom.* See also Muratori, *Ant.-Med. Ævi, Dissert.* 55; and Giulini, *Memor.*, etc., t. ii., p. 151. *Fasti della Chiesa,* vol. vi., p. 153.

BAPTISTERY OF ST. STEPHEN, NEAR ROME.

Leaving Rome by the Porta San Giovanni, the Via Appia Nuova immediately crosses the Mariana stream, and soon after separates from that leading to Frascati. At the second milestone we cross the ancient Via Latina, the direction of which is marked by a line of ruined sepulchres, two of which, in brick, and now converted into temporary farm-buildings, at a short distance on the line, are in good preservation. At this point, and beyond where the modern road intersects the Via Latina, and in the space between them and the Claudian aqueduct, upon the farm of the Arco Travertino, or del Corvo, excavations were made in 1858, which led to the discovery of some most interesting sepulchral monuments of the age of the Antonines, and of the Basilica of St. Stephen, founded in the pontificate of Leo the Great, in the middle of the fifth century. Several marble columns with ancient Composite and Ionic capitals, have been dug out, some of the latter with the cross sculptured on the volutes, and two curious inscriptions, one relative to the foundation of the primitive church by Demetria, a member of the Anician family, the other to the erection of the Bell-Tower by a certain Lupus Grigarius in the middle of the ninth century, thirty years after the rebuilding of the basilica by Pope Leo III. On the right or north-side of this basilica is a square baptistery, with a sunk font in the centre, evidently for baptism by immersion.* In his works, Jacobi Sirmondi makes mention of another baptistery erected in the vicinity of the ancient basilica of St. Paul, on the Ostian way, by Leo the Great in the middle of the fifth century.† This baptistery, which was octagonal in form, is no longer existing.

---

* See *Murray's Handbook for Rome.*
† Jacobi Sirmondi, *Opera Varia*, t. i., col. 1909.

BAPTISTERIES OF RAVENNA.

There are at Ravenna two baptisteries, which are among the most interesting monuments of that city so famed for its edifices of the Roman-Byzantine period. The oldest of these baptisteries is that of San Giovanni in Fonte, which is attached to the original basilica of Ravenna, and is said to have been erected in the fourth century by Orso, Archbishop of that city, and restored by his successor Neon, who adorned it with mosaics, in A. D. 451.* Externally it is a plain octagonal building, surmounted by a circular dome, or cupola. On entering the front door, you find yourself in an octangular hall of about thirty-two feet in diameter. In the centre is a large bath of white Grecian

---

* *Neon* .... *Fontes Ursianiæ Ecclesiæ pulcherrime decoravit, Musivo* .... Agnelli, *Lib. Pontificalis*, part i., p. 237. Isabelle, *Edif. Circulaires*, tav. 42, p. 92. Fabri, *Sagre Memorie di Ravenna antica*, p. 165.

marble, ten feet in diameter, and three and a half feet deep, and provided with an outlet for the purpose of emptying it. Attached to this basin is a marble pulpit, from which the administrator addressed the catechumens before the performance of the rite of baptism.

The cupola is divided into three circles, the smallest of which is the medallion centre of the vault, where the baptism of the Saviour is depicted in mosaics of great magnificence. The Redeemer stands up to his waist in the river Jordan; above him is the dove representing the Holy Ghost; John stands on the bank to the left, one foot raised on a stone, his head erect, and with his right hand he pours the water from a cup on the Saviour's head. With his left he holds a jewelled cross.

Much stress has been laid by Pedobaptist writers on the fact, that in these mosaics, which are of great antiquity, John is represented as *pouring* water on the Saviour's head; therefore, they conclude that baptism in primitive times was administered both by immersion and affusion. It is well to note, however, that the mosaics of this baptistery have been repeatedly restored, and well informed critics are of opinion that unwarrantable additions and alterations have been made in this magnificent work by incompetent artists. These restorations have been rendered necessary by the leaky condition of the cupola, a defect which unfortunately still exists.* The head, right shoulder, and right arm of the Saviour have been restored; and also the head, right shoulder, right arm, and right leg and foot of John the Baptist. Thus we may be indebted to a restorer for the cup, which John holds in his right hand, and the jewelled cross in his left, for in every other painting of the same period, he is represented holding a *reed* in his left hand, and

---

* Cresswell and Casalvasanca, *History of Painting in Italy*, vol. i.

placing his right on the Saviour's head. The mosaics of this famed baptistery have therefore lost much of their archæological value, in consequence of these restorations and alterations.*

The other baptistery was erected by the Arians under the reign of Theodoric, and now forms part of the oratory of the church Santa Maria in Cosmedin. There still remains in the centre a round block of granite, about eight feet and a half in diameter, believed to be a part of the ancient baptismal font. This baptistery has a domical vault, and is supposed to have been adorned with

---

* Paciandus, in his *De Cultu S. Joannis Baptistæ*, attributes these alterations to the ignorance of the painters, who were unacquainted with the historical facts, which they attempted to represent. We quote his own words:

"Numquid Christus omninus *adspersione* baptizatus? Tantum abest a vero, ut nihil magis vero possit esse contrarium, sed errori, et inscientiæ pictorum tribuendum, qui quum historiarum sæpe sunt ignari, vel quia quidlibet audendi potestatem sibi factam credunt, res, quas effigunt, mirifice aliquando depravant."

mosaics after the expulsion of the Goths, which took place in the year A. D. 540. The cupola is divided into circles like that of the earlier baptistery. The same subjects adorn the basin of the dome and the circle immediately beneath it. In the baptism the Saviour is represented youthful and beardless, standing in the Jordan up to his waist; a nimbus surrounds his head, and the dove sheds green rays upon his features. John, on the right, finely shaped, with long hair and beard, holds a reed in his left hand, and places his right on the Saviour's head. The water is level, and not raised into a hillock in the absurd manner afterwards introduced in the middle ages.*

BAPTISTERY OF NAPLES.

The baptistery of Naples is an irregular octagonal building surmounted by a cupola.

---

* D'Agincourt, *Archit.*, tav. 17, Nos. 16 and 63, Nos. 18 and 19. Bellenghi, *Dissertazione su i Battisteri.* Ciampini, *Vetera Monumenta.* Ricci, *Storia dell' Architt. in Italia.*

An old inscription in this baptistery, which is now called San Giovanni in Fonte, supports the tradition that Constantine erected the building in 303. This fact is confirmed by the chronicles of the church Santa Maria del Principio in Villani, but contradicted by Assemanni, a modern writer, who pretends that the erection took place under the auspices of Bishop Vincenzo, between A. D. 556 and 570. The evidence of the mosaics is less favorable to the theory of Assemanni than to the tradition which assigns them to an earlier date.* The mosaics represent four symbolical figures of the Evangelists. St. John in the form of an angel, has the head of an aged man and the regular features of the classic Roman period. In the centre of the cupola is the Greek monogram and cross. Scenes from the life of the Saviour, such at least as might serve to impress the multitude

---

* Catalani, *Le Chiese di Napoli*, vol. ii., pp. 46, 47.

with the idea of his supernatural power and benevolence, adorned the cupola, but are so altered by restoring as to be worthless.

This baptistery is attached to the church of Santa Restituta, the ancient basilica or cathedral of Naples.*

BAPTISTERY OF CITTA NUOVA.

According to a fragment of an inscription found on one of the steps of this baptistery,

Fig. 9.—SECTION AND PLAN OF BAPTISTERY OF CITTA NUOVA IN ISTRIA.

it was erected and adorned by Bishop Mauritius, in the sixth century.† (Fig. 9.) Like the ancient baths it has internally all around

---

* Mazzocchi, *De Cath. Eccl. Nap.*, p. 25 and following.
† Ughelli, *Italia Sacra*, t. v., p. 229.

the building three steps, which rise from the floor. A descent of three steps also leads into the font or basin, which is surrounded by six columns. The diameter of the building is about forty feet, and that of the basin ten feet. The accompanying plans are taken from D'Agincourt's work on architecture. *

BAPTISTERY OF AQUILEJA.

The epoch in which this baptistery was erected is not known with certainty; but that this edifice is of great antiquity is evident from its rustic simplicity, the construction of the basin, which contains three steps all around, and the ancient name this baptistery bore, that of Ecclesia Paganorum. The building was subsequently united to the more modern cathedral, built by Patriarch Poponius, in A. D. 1031.† A good plan of

---

* Agincourt, *Archit.*, pl. lxiii., 13, 14.
† Michael Lopez, *Dissert. su i Battist.*

this baptistery may be seen in Bertoli's well-known work on the antiquities of Aquileja.*

BAPTISTERY OF NOVARA.

Opposite the great door of the Duomo, or Cathedral of Novara, opens the curious octagonal baptistery, supported, as is the case with almost all the very early edifices of the kind, by ancient columns; and hence the tradition, almost invariably annexed to these buildings, of their having been Pagan temples. These columns, of white marble, are fluted and of the Corinthian order, and have originally belonged to an edifice of a good Roman period.† In the centre of the octagonal basin is a circular Roman urn, bearing an inscription to Umbrena Polla, which is as follows:

---

* Bertoli, *Antichità d'Aquileja*. De Rubeis, *Mon. Eccl. Aquil.*

† Murray's *Handbook for Northern Italy.*

VMBRENAE
A. F. POLLAE
DOXA LIBERTA
T. F. I.

This sepulchral urn was formerly used for baptism by immersion.* The large basin, which contains it, and was undoubtedly the original baptismal font, is octagonal in form, and provided with three steps inside and an outlet for the escape of the water. It is about four feet deep and eight feet wide.

BAPTISTERY OF FLORENCE.

The building which is now the Baptistery of Florence has been the subject of much discussion, having by some been considered to be the original temple of Mars; but Lami, in his *Lezioni Toscana*, has set this matter at rest by showing that, though the baptistery is almost entirely composed of antique pillars and marbles, yet, as these

---

* Racca, *Del Duomo e del Battistero di Novada.*

materials are irregularly put together, and as the capitals of the pillars are not the same, this building cannot be Roman work, and must have been constructed in subsequent times.

The exact time at which this edifice was constructed is unknown. That it was a finished building in A. D. 725 is clear from a letter of Speciosus, who was Bishop of Florence at that time, and who speaks of it as his church. Originally this building was not the baptistery, but the cathedral. It stood without the walls, but in those times it was not unusual for cathedrals to be so placed. In the thirteenth century, the citizens of Florence determined to have a cathedral on a larger scale, and when this was accomplished, St. John's became the baptistery.*

Originally, like the Pantheon at Rome,

---

* Knight, *Church Architecture of Italy*. Ricca, *Notiz. delle Chies. Fior.*

BAPTISM AND BAPTISTERIES. 141

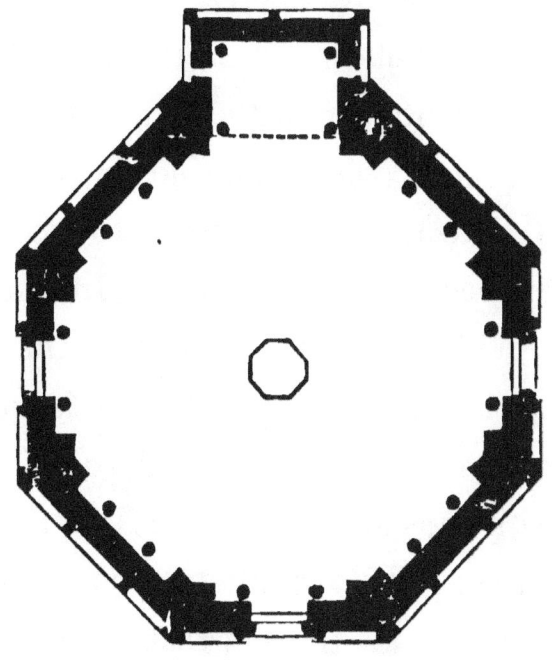

Fig. 10.—PLAN OF BAPTISTERY AT FLORENCE.

this building was open at the top. It was secured from the weather * in 1150, but the mosaics of the dome were not added till 1225.

This celebrated baptistery is an octagonal structure (Fig. 10), measuring about one

---

* Lami, *Index Chronologicus*.

hundred feet in diameter. It stands detached from, but in the immediate vicinity of the Duomo, or cathedral. It is built of black and white marble in the style which Giotto is said to have introduced, and which is peculiar to Tuscany. Internally a gallery, which runs nearly round the whole building, is supported by sixteen large granite columns, and the vaulted roof is decorated with mosaics by Andrea Tafi, the pupil of Cimabue. This baptistery is celebrated especially for its three great bronze doors with their beautiful bas-reliefs. Two of these doors, sculptured by Ghiberti, were immortalised by Michael Angelo with the name of Gates of Paradise.*

On the pavement of the baptistery is a large circle of copper, with numerical figures and signs of the zodiac upon it, and in the centre of this stood originally a very fine oc-

---

* Sgrilli, *Descrizione del Battistero di Firenze.*

Baptism and Baptisteries.
Interior of Baptistery of Florence.

tangular basin of a diameter of twelve feet. This large font was destroyed by Francesco de' Medici upon the occasion of the baptism of his son Philip, in 1576, greatly to the displeasure of the Florentines, who carried away, as relics, the fragments of marble and mortar.*

In his immortal work on the *Inferno*, the poet Dante speaks of this building "*mio bel San Giovanni*," as if he delighted in it, though his mischance in breaking some part of the baptismal font for the purpose of saving some one from drowning, occasioned one of the many unjust charges for which he suffered during his troubled life. Speaking of the cavities in which sinners guilty of simony are punished, he compares them to the fonts: †

---

* Ricca, *Notiz. delle Chiese Fiorent.*, t. v., part. I. Lami, *Lezioni di Antich. Toscane*, tom. i., lez. 5a.

† Murray's *Handbook for Italy*.

> ". . . . . Nel mio bel San Giovanni,
> Fatti per luogo de' battezzatori;
> L'un degli quali, ancor non è molt' anni,
> Rupp' io per un che dentro v'annegava:
> E questo sia suggel ch'ogni uomo sganni." .
> <div align="right">(<i>Inf.</i> xix., 17–21.)</div>

> ". . . . . In St. John's fair fane, by me beloved,
> Those basins formed for water, to baptize:
> One of the same I broke some years ago,
> To save a drowning person; be this my word;
> A seal, the motive of my deed to show."
> <div align="right">(<i>Wright's Dante.</i>)</div>

It is not known to a certainty which font it was that the poet broke, for it appears that the Baptistery of Florence was provided with a number of fonts, where, at Easter, baptism was administered by immersion.

BAPTISTERY OF BOLOGNA.

No record remains of the origin, or date, of the circular church of San Stephano; but the most probable hypothesis appears to be, that it was the ancient baptistery of Bologna, and that it was built either by the Lombard king Luitprandus,* or by the people of Bologna, in the eighth century.† In the immediate vicinity of this building stands a church, of which the predecessor was the original Cathedral of Bologna, near to which, about the year 430, St. Petronius, who was at that time Bishop of Bologna, built the monastery of San Stephano, which afterwards gave its name to the whole region.‡ The monastery and the church were almost entirely destroyed by the Hungarians in A. D. 903, but were rebuilt about a century afterwards. The baptistery appears to have escaped with little injury. After the Crusades, and when the baptismal rite was transferred to the church, the baptistery was converted into a chapel of the Holy Sepulchre, for which destination it was already adapted by its circular form.

---

* Hope, *History of Architecture*, Italian edition, p. 106.
† Ricci, *Stor. dell' Architt.*, t. i., p. 239. Bianconi, *Della Chiesa del S. Sapolero.*
‡ Sigonius, *Hist. Bononiensis.*

The name of Luitprandus is associated with this building on account of a large marble basin, which is yet to be seen in the court of the adjacent church, and which bears an inscription in which the name of Luitprandus appears. But there is no evidence to show whether he built the whole edifice, or only presented it with a font; and the short time during which he was in possession of Bologna (which in those days formed a part of the Exarchate of Ravenna), makes the latter more probable than the former.*

BAPTISTERY OF VERONA.

This baptistery was rebuilt in A. D. 1135 by Bishop Bernando, the older building having been destroyed by an earthquake in 1116. In the centre is a large octangular basin of marble, twenty-eight feet in circumference,

---

* Knight, *Architecture in Italy*.

hewn out of a single block of Venetian marble.* By actual measurement, we found the depth of this font to be four feet and a half. A frieze of small Lombard arches supported by grotesque heads, runs round the summit. On the faces are represented the following subjects: The Annunciation, the Visitation, the Birth of our Lord, the Angels appearing to the Shepherds, the Adoration of the Wise Men,

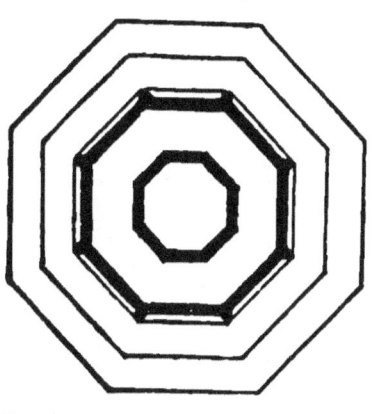

Fig. 11.—PLAN OF BAPTISTERY AT VERONA.

Fig. 12.—ELEVATION OF BAPTISTERY AT VERONA.

Herod commanding the Slaughter of the Innocents, the Execution of his Decree, the

---

* Maffei, *Verona Illustrata*, part iii., cap. 3.

Flight into Egypt, the Baptism of Christ in the Jordan. In the last-mentioned subject, the water of the Jordan is raised into a hillock, and our Saviour is being immersed in it. Two angels stand on the shore holding his garments. There is also a picture of the baptism of Christ over the high altar.

BAPTISTERY OF CIVIDALE.

Cividale, in the Province of Venetia, the ancient Forum Julii, is interesting from its numerous Roman antiquities. Its Duomo, or Collegiate Church, founded in A. D. 750, is a remarkable mediæval edifice, and contains a handsome baptismal font. It is an octagonal basin, four feet and a half in diameter, and three feet deep, and was formerly used for the administration of baptism by immersion. This elegant font stood in former times in the centre of the baptistery erected near the cathedral by Callixtus, Bishop of Aquileja, in A. D. 737. But after the destruction of the building, which took place in 1645, the font was transferred to the church, where it is still to be seen. It is surrounded by eight columns elegantly sculptured, which support semi-circular arches, adorned with figures, symbols, and various inscriptions.*

BAPTISTERY OF ASCOLI.

On the north side of the cathedral there is a detached baptistery, a building of the ninth or tenth century. It is square at the base and octagonal above. Recent excavations † have brought to light a large circular basin, built of travertine marble, and which stood in the middle of the baptistery. To it was attached a square pulpit, from which the administrator addressed the catechumens

---

* Zancarol, *Ant. Civ. For. Jul.*, lib. iii. De Rubeis, *Eccl. Aquil. Mon.* Del Torre, *Latt. Intorno alle Ant. Crist.*

† Orsini, *Descrizione delle Pitt. Ecc. della Città di Ascoli.* Lazzari, *Ascoli in Prospettiva.*

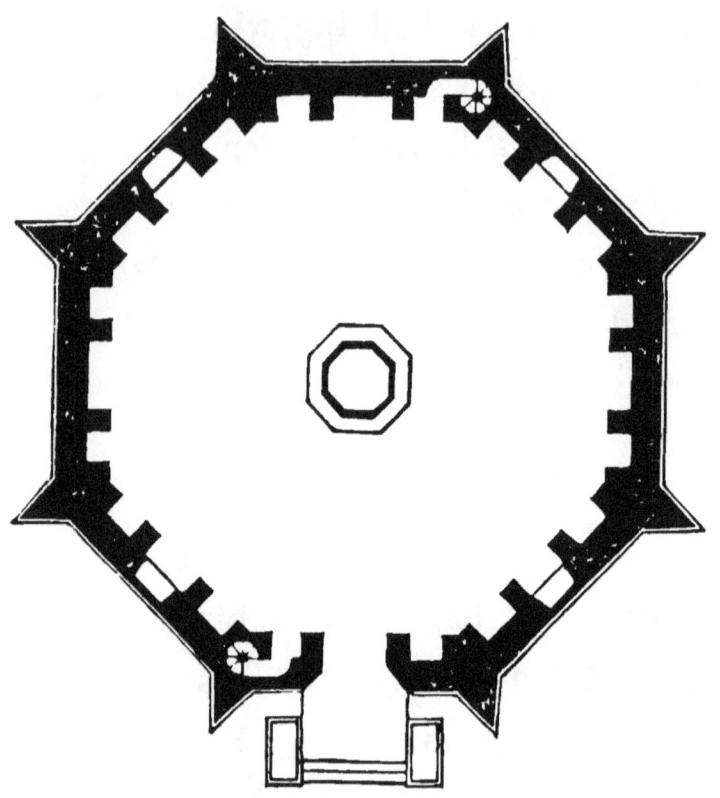

Fig. 13.—PLAN OF BAPTISTERY OF CREMONA.

previous to admitting them to the rite of baptism.* The style of the whole building is Byzantine.

BAPTISTERY OF CREMONA.

Neither ancient nor modern writers agree in determining the epoch of the construction

---

* Lopez, *Battisteri*, p. 269.

Baptism and Baptisteries.
The Baptistery of Cremona.

Page 151.

of the magnificent Baptistery of Cremona, but it is generally thought to be not much posterior to the tenth century. The building is octagonal, about sixty feet in diameter, and has sixteen columns of Veronese marble, which support the roof and cupola. (Fig. 13.) In the centre is a large octagonal marble basin of a diameter of six feet.* The building is in a plain and simple Lombard style. It has, what is very rare in this class of edifices, a fine projecting porch, supported by lions. The windows, by which it is scantily lighted, might serve for a Norman castle. The walls within are covered with ranges of Lombard arches, and fragments of frescoes are seen in the gloom.†

BAPTISTERY OF TORCELLO.

Torcello was the parent island of the Venetian States; the spot to which the unfor-

---

* Merula, *Santuario di Cremona.* Aporti, *Eccl. Crem.*
† Murray's *Handbook for Italy.*

tunate inhabitants of Altinum and Aquileja fled for safety when their homes were made desolate by the northern invaders. Thus peopled, Torcello became a town, and had its cathedral and its bishops long before the existence of St. Mark's at Venice. The cathedral stands in the same state in which it was rebuilt in the beginning of the eleventh century, by Orso Orseolo, Bishop of Torcello, and son of the celebrated Doge Pietro Orseolo.

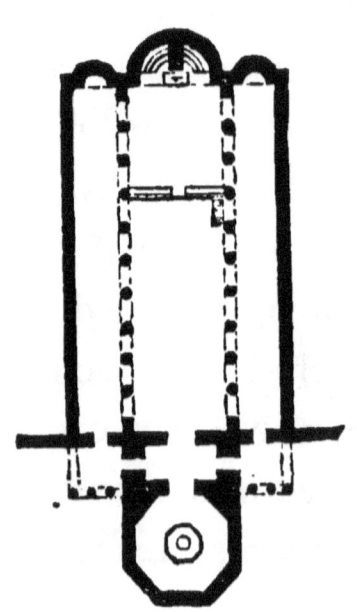

Fig. 14.—PLAN OF CATHEDRAL AND BAPTISTERY OF TORCELLO.

In front of the west door of the cathedral may still be traced the remains of a very perfect baptistery. (Fig. 14.) This was a square building externally, measuring thirty-seven feet each way; and internally an octagon, with the angles cut into hemispherical niches. In the centre stood a large font in the form of a Greek cross, with semi-circular sides.*

BAPTISTERY OF PADUA.

This baptistery is said to have been built about the middle of the twelfth century, although Italian authors disagree as to the precise time in which it was founded. All agree, however, in stating that it was finished and adorned in A. D. 1376. The building is square at the base and circular above. In the centre stands a large circular font, five feet across, and four feet deep. It was formerly used for immersion.

BAPTISTERY OF PISA.

This magnificent baptistery has deservedly excited the admiration of travellers. It was begun in A. D. 1153; Diotisalvi was the name

---

* Costadoni, *Osservazioni Intorno la Chiesa Catted. di Torcello*, p. 33.

of the architect,* but he did not bring the work to a conclusion. It remained unfinished a number of years, from a deficiency of funds. At length, the citizens of Pisa levied a rate for the purpose. An inscription on the south side of the interior, near the floor of the gallery, cut deep in the circular wall, indicates that the work was resumed in 1278. There is reason to believe from the date on the monument of an operarius, or builder, within the fabric, that it was not completed before the fourteenth century; all which sufficiently accounts for the finials and ornaments in the pointed style, which appear in the upper parts of the building.†

This baptistery is of singular design. The plan is circular, with a diameter of one hun-

---

* The following inscriptions are found on two pilasters within the building:

MCLIII MENSE AVG. FVNDATA FVIT HEC ECCLESIA.
DEO TI SALVI MAGISTER HVIVS OPERIS.

† Knight, *Ecclesiastical Architecture of Italy*. Morona, *Pisa Illustrata*.

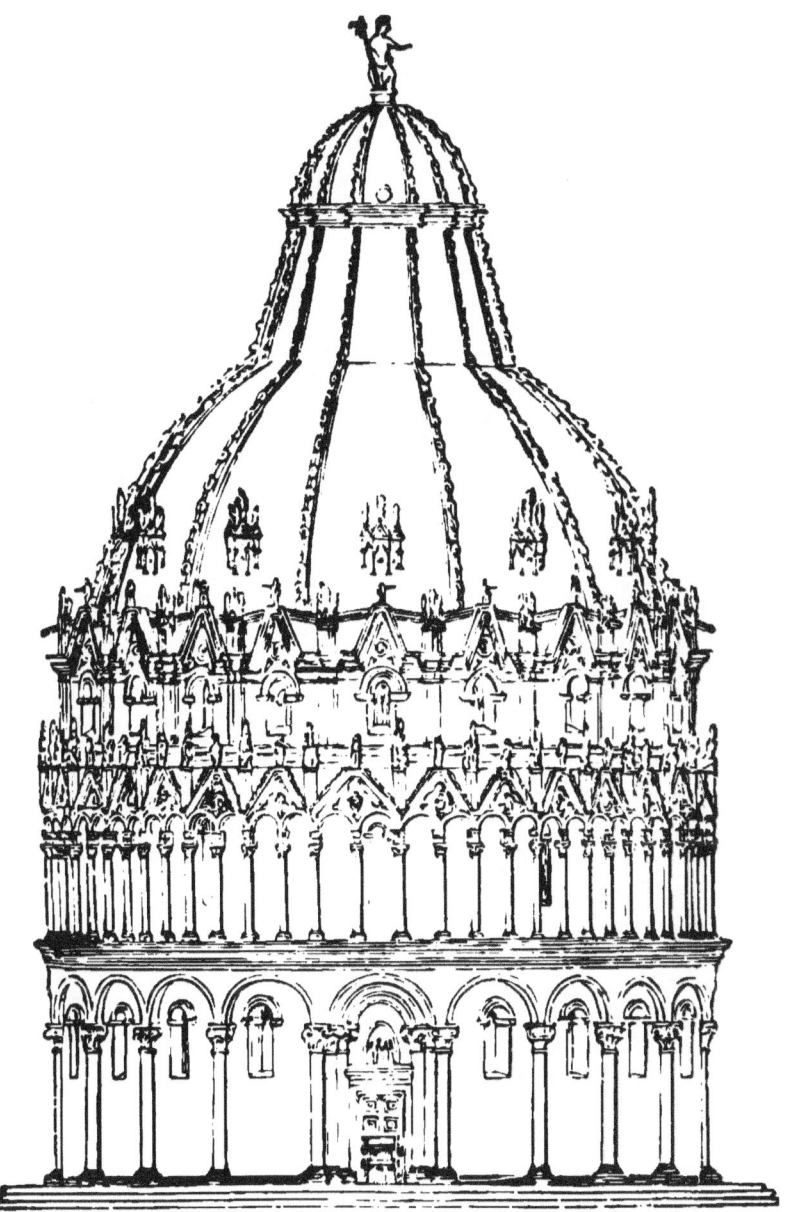

Baptism and Baptisteries.

The Baptistery of Pisa.

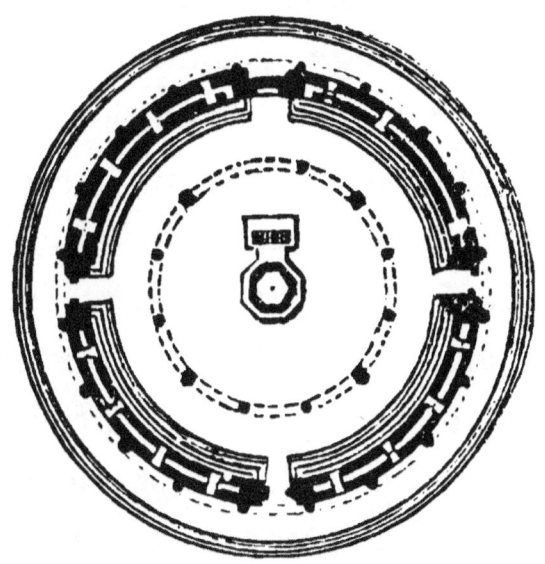

Fig. 15.—PLAN OF BAPTISTERY AT PISA.

dred and sixteen feet; the walls are eight feet thick, the building is raised on three steps, and surmounted with a dome in the shape of a pear. (Fig. 15.) The external elevation is divided into three stories; in the basement the columns, twenty in number, are *engaged*, and have arches springing from column to column, with a bold cornice above. In the first story the columns are smaller, stand out in relief, and are placed closer together, and the order is surmounted with pinnacles and high pediments, placed at equal distances: the terminations of these parts are crowned with statues. Above this is an attic story, decorated with other high pediments, pinnacles, and statues. The dome, which is covered with lead, is intersected by long lines of very prominent fretwork; all the lines meet in a little cornice near the top, and terminate in another dome, above which is a statue of John the Baptist. The interior is much admired for its proportions; light columns of granite, placed between four piers decorated with pilasters, are arranged round the basement story, which support a second order of piers, arranged in a similar manner, on which the dome rests. This dome is famous for its echo, as the sides produce the well-known effect of whispering galleries.*

---

* Encyclopædia, Article *Baptistery*. Milani, *Battistero di Pisa*. Isabelle, *Edif. Circulaires*.

The principal entrance, facing the east and the duomo, is by a decorated doorway, and there is a descent of three steps round the building; the space between the steps and the wall was provided for the accommodation of the persons assembled to witness the ceremony of baptism.

In the centre of the baptistery is a large octagonal basin, fourteen feet in diameter, and four feet deep. It is provided with an outlet for the escape of the water. The basin can be filled by means of a tube connected with a pump outside of the building. At the alternate sides of the font are four small conical basins, which are supposed to have been used when baptism by immersion was practised.* But what was their particular purpose, we have been unable to ascertain.

---

* Michael Lopez, *Sopra i Battisteri.*

BAPTISTERY OF PARMA.

The baptistery at Parma was commenced in A. D. 1196, and constructed after the designs of Benedetto Antelmi.* But the work experienced many interruptions, especially during the supremacy of the powerful and ferocious Ezzelino da Romana, who, in the middle of the thirteenth century, governed the North of Italy in the name of the Emperor, and who, displeased with the inhabitants of Parma, forbade them access to the quarries of the Veronese territory, from which the marble with which the baptistery was built was obtained.† In consequence of these interruptions, the building was not

---

* Upon the architrave of the northern door of the baptistery is the following inscription :

BIS: BINIS: DEMPTIS   INCEPIT: DICTUS:
ANNIS: DE MILLE   OPUS: HOC: SCULTOR
DUCENTIS: BENEDICTUS:

† *Storia della Città di Parma di Angelo Pezzana.* *Thesaurus Ecclesiæ, Parmensis.* Affò, *Storia di Parma.*

finished before 1281; which will sufficiently account for the appearance of the round style in the lower part of the building, and of the pointed, above. Externally, this baptistery is an octagon, six stories in height, ending in a dome, which is covered by a flat wooden roof. The lowest and the highest stories are solid, the others are galleries supported by small columns. The interior has sixteen sides, from which spring converging ribs, that form a pointed dome. The portals are enriched with mouldings and pillars, but without imagery. In the interior of the baptistery the walls are ornamented with frescoes of the thirteenth century; meagerly executed, but well preserved.*

In the centre stands a very large octagonal basin, cut out from one block of yellowish-red marble. It appears from an in-

---

* Knight's *Ecclesiastical Architecture of Italy.*

scription* cut on the rim that this font was made by Johannes Pallassonus in 1299. It is about eight feet in diameter, four feet deep, and contains another basin in the form of a Greek cross, in which the administrator stood during the performance of the rite.† That this font was formerly used for baptism by immersion, is clearly attested by the following extract, taken from the official report forwarded to the Pope on November 21st, 1578, in which is given a full description of the baptistery and its uses. This report is still preserved in the church records of Parma. The extract is as follows:

"In eadem Ecclesia adest Baptisterium, et adsunt fontes separati a Baptisterio.

"Ad sacri fontis consecrationem parochi Civitatis non conveniunt.

---

* The following is the inscription:
MCCLXXXXVIIII
JOHANES DE PALLASONO I.ᵃ P̄P̄.ᵃ

† Michael Lopez, *Battistero di Parma*, p. 161. His description of this baptistery is very complete.

"Officium baptizandi pertinet ad duos sacerdotes qui appellantur *Dogmani;* attamen ipsi non baptizant, sed habent substitutum qui eorum vices supplet.

"Baptizant per immersionem."

In one corner of the baptistery is a smaller font, or, at least, what is now used as such, covered with Runic foliage and strange animals; it stands upon a lion setting his paws upon a ram. All the children born in Parma are now brought to this font to be sprinkled, a practice which was introduced after the sixteenth century, and mentioned for the first time in 1622.*

On the pilasters and lunette of the northern gate are carved the roots of Jesse and of Joachim, and scenes from the life of the Saviour and John the Baptist. In the baptism they are both represented standing up to the middle in the waters of the Jordan, which are raised into a hillock in the absurd man-

---

* Michael Lopez, *Battistero di Parma*, p. 120.

Fig. 16.—BAPTISM OF CHRIST IN JORDAN. A BAS RELIEF IN THE BAPTISTERY OF PARMA; 13th CENTURY.

ner so generally adopted in the middle ages. A sketch of this sculpture is presented in the accompanying woodcut.* (Fig. 16.)

In the third course of the dome are also scenes from the life of John the Baptist, amongst which one, the Baptism of Christ, was represented in a form which is but an amplification of that adopted in the Catacomb of San Ponziano at Rome. The Redeemer is placed in the middle of a running stream; John on the right bank places his hand on the Saviour's head; on the left bank stand three angels holding his clothes. The scene is repeated in a second baptism on the wall behind the altar. It is almost obliterated.

---

* Michael Lopez, *Battistero di Parma*, p. 170.

BAPTISTERY OF PISTOIA.

This baptistery stands opposite the Cathedral of Pistoia, and is called San Giovanni Rotondo, although it is an octagon in shape. According to Vasari, this building was erected in the year 1337 by Andrea Pisano. The style of the exterior is Italian-Gothic. The walls are covered with black and white marble in alternate layers, and surrounded by columns decorated with mosaics.

The interior of the baptistery is bare and without decoration, and in its primitive simplicity presents a pleasing contrast with the profuse artistic and idolatrous display so universal in Italy. In the centre stands a large square basin, ten feet in diameter, and four feet deep, which can contain about nine barrels of water, according to information kindly furnished by an ecclesiastic attached to the cathedral. This font, which is of fine marble, is said to be older than the present building, probably of 1256.

BAPTISTERY OF ST. PETER'S AT ROME.

In the chapel of the baptistery, the first on the left of this magnificent basilica, there is an ancient vase of red porphyry, which formed the cover of the tomb of the Emperor Otho II., as it did more anciently that of Hadrian, and which now serves as a baptismal font. When the church was erected this font was raised on three marble steps,[*] but Benedictus XIII., elected Pope in 1724, being anxious to conform to the ancient rite of administering baptism by immersion, ordered the construction of two steps below the pavement, forming thus a large basin, in which adult persons could be immersed with ease. Now, that the primitive rite is definitively abandoned, this basin is partly closed with a wooden pavement.[†] A commemora-

---

[*] Martinelli, *Basilica Vaticana*, lib. ii., p. 116.
[†] Valentini, *Basilica Vaticana*, t. ii.

tive inscription, engraved in gilded letters on a marble slab beneath the large picture in rear of the font, reads as follows:

BENEDICTVS XIII. PONT. MAX.
ORD. PRÆDICATORVM.
HVMANÆ REGENERATIONIS FONTEM
VETERI RITV INSTAVRAVIT
ANNO SAL. MDCCXXV.
PONT. SVI ANNO II.

THE END.

INDEX.

ABLUTION, a common religious rite, 12.
   used in worship of Mithra, Egyptians, and Greeks, 12.
Alcuinus, 23.
Alcuinus Avitus, 47.
Ambrosius, Archbishop of Milan, 21, 125.
Anastasius, 114, 116, 121.
Andrea Pisano erects the Baptistery of Pistoia, A. D. 1337, 163.
Andrea Tafi, 142.
Apostolical Constitutions, 38, 78, 81, 87, 89, 98.
Aqua Lustralis, see Water of Purification.
Aquinas, Thomas, 52.
Assemanni, 135.
Audientes, see Catechumens.
Augustine, 27, 31, 44, 83, 84, 87, 89, 126.

Baptism:
   administrators of, 77, 109.
   bas-reliefs of, 61, 148, 161, 162.
   of Christ, picture of, at Verona, 148.
   Christian, what it requires, 19.
   clinic, 78, 97.
   forms and ceremonies accompanying, 64, 66.
   import of, 20, 21, 22, 23.

Baptism:
   instituted by Christ, 17.
   of Jewish proselytes, 15.
   John's, 17.
   Justin Martyr on, 34.
   lay baptism, 71.
   mode of administering, 53, 103, 131.
   ordinary mode in primitive church, 33.
   pagan, 13.
   a perpetual ordinance, 19.
   required by apostles, 18.
   Russian, 61.
   a symbol, 19.
   Tertullian on, 36.
   of Theodosius the younger, 72.
   times for, 74, 89, 106, 109.
   of Valerian, 61.
   where administered, 100.
   who admitted to, 83.
Baptisteries:
   at Aquileja, 137.
   Ascoli, 149.
   Bologna, 144.
   Catacomb of San Ponziano, 102.
   Città Nuova, 136.
   Cividale, 148.
   Cremona, 150.
   Florence, 139.
   Milan, 125.
   San Giovanni alle Fonte, 126.

INDEX.

Baptisteries:
  San Stefano alle Fonte, 126.
  in Milan Cathedral, 127.
  Naples, 134.
  Nocera dei Pagani, 123.
  Novara, 138.
  Padua, 153.
  Parma, 158.
  Pisa, 153.
  Pistoia, 162.
  Ravenna, 130.
  San Giovanni in Fonte, 130.
  Santa Maria in Cosmedin, 133.
  Rome:
    of Constantine, 106, 112.
    of St. Costanza, 119.
    of St. Peters, 164.
    of St. Stephen, 128.
  Torcello, 151.
  Verona, 146.
  derivation of word, 106.
  internal arrangement, 108.
  list of, in Italy, 110.
  shape, 106.
  situation and size, 109.
Basil. 44, 77, 79.
Bas Reliefs, 148, 161, 162.
  in baptistery at Verona, 147.
Bathing:
  at Eleusinian mysteries, 12.
  by priests, 12.
  of Proselytes, by Jews, 15.
Bede, 27, 48.
Benedetto Antelmi designs baptistery at Parma, 158.
Benedictus XIII. (1725) prepares font at Rome for immersion, 164.
Bernard, 51.
Beroldus, 127.
Bishop Bernardo rebuilds baptistery of Verona, A. D. 1135, 146.
Bottari, 103.
Bugati, 59.

Callixtus builds baptistery at Cividale, A. D. 737, 148.
Catacombs:
  baptisteries in, 102.
  sepulchral chapels in, 96.

Catacombs:
  paintings in, 24, 25, 28, 54, 102.
  water, how obtained, 105.
Catechists:
  apostles' creed used by, 94.
  office of, 94.
  place for instruction, 95.
Catechumenate, duration of, 97.
Catechumens:
  first class, Audientes, or hearers, 87.
  second class, Genuflectentes, or kneelers, 87,
  third class, Competenti, or Electi, 88.
  examination of, 90.
  females taught by deaconesses, 93.
  going veiled, 91.
  learn the creed, 91.
Celestine, Pope, 52.
Ceremonies:
  anointing, 67, 68, 69.
  attendants clothed in white, 71, 72.
  bread given with milk and honey, 73.
  candles, 73.
  insufflation, 67.
  kiss of peace, 73, 80.
  milk and honey given, 68, 73, 82.
  turning to the East, 66.
  washing the feet, 74, 82.
  wearing white garments, 69, 75.
Chrysostom, 20, 69, 73, 78, 79.
Ciampini, 61.
Clemens Alexandrinus, 13, 29.
Clement of Rome, 38.
Communion, 79.
  none but believers and baptized partake, 81.
Competenti, or Electi, see Catechumens.
Constantine, Emperor, 105, 113, 135.
Cyprian, 40, 43, 68.
Cyril of Jerusalem, 42, 56, 65, 66, 68, 88.

Dante, 143.

Deaconesses teach female catechumens, 93.
    qualifications of, 93.
Dionysius, 34.
Diotisalvi, architect of baptistery of Pisa, 153.
Diptych at San Celso, Milan, 59.
Doctor Audientium, 92.

Epiphanius, 44.
Eunodius, 126.
Eusebius, 42, 83.
Exorcism preceding baptism, 64, 65, 68.
Ezzelino da Romana, 158.

Fish:
    figurative designation of our Lord, 29, 30, 33.
    symbol of baptism and the Lord's Supper, 28.
Fonts:
    at Ascoli, 149.
    baptistery of Constantine, 116, 119.
    Cividale, 147.
    Cremona, 151.
    Milan, 127.
    Padua, 153.
    Parma, 159, 161.
    St. Peter's, Rome, 164.
    Pisa, 157.
    Pistoia, 163.
    Ravenna, 133.
    Torcello, 153
    Verona, 147.
Frigidarium at Pompeii, 107.

Ganges, Hindoo reverence for, 15.
Genuflectentus, see Catechumens.
Ghiberti, artist of bronze doors at Florence, 142.
Giotto, 142.
Gregory the Great, 22, 70.
Gregory of Nazianzen, 26, 78.
Gregory of Nyssa, 20, 77, 78, 89.
Gregory Thaumaturgus, 41

Herodotus, 12.
Hesychius, 12.
Hilary, 30.
Honorius Augustus, 101.

Ignatius, 73.
Immersion, simple, 49.
    trine, 35, 37, 38, 43, 44, 45, 47, 49, 52, 63, 82.
Import of baptism:
    Ambrosius on, 21.
    Chrysostom on, 20.
    Gregory the Great on, 22.
    Gregory of Nyssa on, 20.
    Justin Martyr on, 20.
    Maximus on, 22.
    Theodulphus on, 23.
    Theodulus on, 21.
Inscription, discovered near Autun, 31.
    in baptistery at Cividale, 149.
    Naples, 135.
    Novara, 139.
    Pisa, 154.
    St. Peter's, Rome, 165.
    basilica of St. Stephen, 129.
    church at Bologna, 146.
    Città Nuova, 136.
Insufflation, 67.
Irenæus, 35.
Isidore, 50.

Jacobi Sirmondi, 129.
Jerome, 29, 70, 77.
John's baptism, 17, 100.
Justin Martyr, 20, 33, 79, 100.
Justinian, Emperor, 98.
Juvencus, 45.

Lactantius, 41.
Leo the Great, 47.
Leo Isaurian, Emperor of Constantinople, 95.
Leo of Modena, 16.
Luitprandus, 145, 146.

Marcus Gazensis, 71.
Maximus, Bishop of Turin, 22, 47.
Melito, 30.
Mosaics in baptistery of St. Costanza, 120.
    Florence, 142.
    Ravenna, 130, 131.

Names of the faithful, 84, 85.

Optatus, 30.

Oratory of St. Venantius, 96.
Origen, 39, 64.
Orso Orseolo, Bishop of Torcello, rebuilds the Cathedral, 152.

Paintings of Baptism in Basilica of St. Clement, 56.
  Catacombs, 25, 54, 103.
  Ciclo Biblico, 24.
  Church of San Lorenzo, Rome, 103.
  Hotel de Ville, Rheims, 62.
  Miniature in ancient manuscript, 58.
        at Verona, 162.
Pallassonus, Johannes, makes font at Parma, A. D. 1299, 160.
Paulinus, 48, 101.
Photizomenoi, or the illuminated, 88.
Pliny, 106.
Prosper, 27.
Prudentius, 46.
Pulpit:
  in baptistery at Ascoli, 149.
        Ravenna, 131.

Red Sea, passage of, a figure of baptism, 26, 27.
Rossi, Signor, 24.

San Giovanni in Fonte, Rome, 113.
San Giovanni alle Fonte, Milan, 126.
Saturnus, 37.

Seneca, 117.
Severus, Alexandrinus, 67.
Socrates, 99, 109.
Sprinkling of children in font at Parma, 161.
  of water of Purification, 14.
  over food at religious repasts, 14.
St. Petronius builds monastery at Bologna, A. D. 430, 145.
Symbols of Baptism, 24, 25, 26, 28.

Tertullian, 13, 24, 30, 36, 53, 64, 65, 68, 74, 77, 82, 101.
Theodoret, 14.
Theodorus of Mopsuestia, 92.
Theodulphus, 23.
Theodulus of Cœle-syria, 21.
Theophilus, 35.
Trine Immersion, its import, 21, 23.

Unction, 67, 69.

Valerian, baptism of, 61.
Venantius Fortunatus, 71.

Walafrid Strabon, 101.
Warnefridus, Paulus, 71.
Water of Purification, 14.
  sprinkled on worshippers in the Roman temples, 14.
  used in forum, 14.
    in funeral rites, 14.
    by Jews, 15.

THE END.

www.ingramcontent.com/pod-product-compliance
Lightning Source LLC
Chambersburg PA
CBHW020304170426
43202CB00008B/491